■ SCHOLASTIC

Reteaching Math

GEOMETRY & MEASUREMENT

Mini-Lessons, Games & Activities to Review
& Reinforce Essential Math Concepts & Skills

Denise Birrer, Stephanie DiLorenzo & Bob Krech

New York • Toronto • London • Auckland • Sydney
Mexico City • New Delhi • Hong Kong • Buenos Aires

Teaching *Resources*

DEDICATION

For Beth, Mas, and Jack
—DB and SD

ACKNOWLEDGMENTS

We'd like to acknowledge Bob for giving us this opportunity. Thanks for being a
wonderful mentor, editor, and coauthor. We truly admire all you do.
—DB and SD

Editor: Mela Ottaiano
Cover design by Brian LaRossa
Interior design by Holly Grundon
Interior illustrations by Mike Moran

ISBN-13: 978-0-439-52968-6
ISBN-10: 0-439-52968-9

Table of Contents

Table of Contents (continued)

REPRODUCIBLE STUDENT PAGES

Introduction

Most math books that have the word *reteaching* in the title typically feature many pages of equations and practice problems. The reasoning may be that if students need a concept or skill to be retaught, the best way for them to gain mastery is to practice more of the same. Research does show that some students need more time on a task than other students in order to learn a concept. However, if a student does not understand a concept or skill the first time, presenting a series of problems that the student already finds difficult and repeating them, without new knowledge or intervention, will most likely not be successful.

To reteach implies actually teaching again, not merely repeated practice. Students need to have a strong conceptual understanding if they are going to be able to do mathematics with accuracy and comprehension. Without this understanding, math can become meaningless and students simply work by rote. That's why we've created the Reteaching Math series. You will find this series is different from most reteaching books in that the emphasis is on helping students develop understanding as well as providing useful practice.

Using a Problem Solving Approach

The activities, games, and lessons in this book are just plain good instruction, with an emphasis on solving problems and applying math in context. Problem solving is the first process standard listed in the NCTM *Principles and Standards for School Mathematics* (2000). The accompanying statement reads, "Problem solving should be the central focus of all mathematics instruction and an integral part of all mathematical activity." In other words, problem solving is what math is all about. Every lesson here begins with a problem to solve to help create a spirit of inquiry and interest. Practice problems are integrated into the lessons so they are meaningful. Real reteaching!

Providing Context

It is important to provide students with a context to help give learning mathematical skills and concepts meaning. Context helps learners understand how these mathematical ideas and tools are useful and can be applied to real-life problems and situations. Context can be provided by creating a theme that carries throughout all the lessons. In this book, the theme of Super Space Stations, Inc. gives the students a context in which learning about geometry and measurement is relevant, motivating, and fun. The use of the overarching space theme gives all the lessons a sense of cohesion and purpose.

What's Inside?

Activity Lessons – introduce major concepts and skills. Timed to last about 40 minutes, these lessons are designed to help students work on the ideas in a hands-on manner and context to help them understand the meaning behind the math and give them an opportunity to apply it in a fun way.

Practice Pages – specially designed to provide both practice and a helpful reference sheet for students. Each practice page begins with a word problem so students can see how and why the math is useful in solving real problems. Each page also features a **Basics Box**. Here, concepts are carefully presented with words, numbers, pictures, definitions, and step-by-step explanations. **Example problems** help solidify understanding, then a series of problems give students practice. Finally, a **journal prompt** helps students discuss and explore the concept using pictures, numbers, and words, while providing you with an additional assessment opportunity that looks at student thinking and understanding. Practice pages can be worked on together in class, assigned to be done independently, or even given as homework assignments.

Review Pages – provide students with additional focused practice on a specific math concept. The concept is practiced in a variety of formats and is designed to be completed independently. In addition, to practice on the focus concept a mixed review of concepts introduced earlier is included on each Review Page. By spiraling the curriculum in this way, students' retention and recall of math ideas is supported. These pages may be used for review, practice, homework, or assessment of students' knowledge and understanding.

Addressing Various Learning Styles

A good way to help all students learn mathematics well is to present ideas through physical, pictorial, and symbolic representations. Research suggests the importance of learning math through modeling with manipulatives. Math concepts need to be experienced on a physical level before pictorial and more abstract representations can be truly understood. Relying completely on symbolic representations (e.g., lots of equations) is not enough, particularly in a reteaching situation.

Learning experiences featured here include using manipulatives, drawing pictures, writing equations, reading stories, and playing games to help learners gain strong conceptual knowledge.

About Geometry and Measurement

Humans have used the concepts of geometry and measurement to build the world around us. As we begin to notice shapes and structures, we also recognize the space that they take up in the two- and three-dimensional realm. To help students develop an understanding of these ideas they need hands-on experiences. Students should be given opportunities to measure actual objects so they will be able to estimate, make appropriate choices about which measures to use, and understand how different measures are related. As students internalize these concepts through experience, they learn to solve problems in which measurement and geometry ideas are presented in a more abstract manner.

Similarly, when learning geometry concepts, it is important for students to have hands-on experience manipulating shapes. A student who has actually handled a cube is more likely to be able to visualize its faces when asked to recognize them from an abstract drawing or an unseen object. Students should be given time to explore the attributes of different shapes and learn how they are related so that they can solve problems presented in an abstract manner. When students are given opportunities to see how their lives are influenced by geometry and measurement and are provided with actual experiences in using these concepts, they are able to develop a more complete understanding of the underlying ideas.

How to Use This Book

This book can be used as a replacement unit, as a resource for activities for math workshops or centers, or a supplement to find engaging ideas to enhance a textbook unit. The lessons and activities are presented in a developmental sequence, but can be used effectively as stand-alone or supplementary learning experiences. Since it's written to accommodate all learners, you can use it to teach a unit on geometry and measurement to any class.

The NCTM Standards for geometry and measurement include the following expectations for grades 2–4:
- identify, compare, and analyze attributes of two- and three-dimensional shapes
- classify two- and three-dimensional shapes according to their properties and recognize related shapes
- investigate, describe, and reason about the results of putting together and taking apart two- and three-dimensional shapes
- explore congruence and line and rotational symmetry
- describe location and movement
- make and use coordinate systems and find the distances between points
- predict and describe the results of sliding, flipping, and turning
- build and draw two- and three-dimensional shapes and recognize how they are related in creating each other
- use geometric models, ideas, and relationships to solve problems
- recognize the attributes of length, area, volume, and perimeter
- understand how to measure using standard and nonstandard measurements and the need for standard units as utilized by the customary and metric systems
- calculate simple conversions within a system of measurement

- select an appropriate unit and tool for the attribute being measured and use it effectively
- select and use benchmarks to estimate measurements
- understand and utilize strategies for calculating area and volume of selected shapes

Within these expectations are more specific objectives. These are addressed in the learning experiences throughout this book and include:
- describe, identify, create, and compare two- and three-dimensional shapes using pictures and objects
- recognize and classify two- and three-dimensional shapes according to their structure and how they are related to each other
- investigate combining shapes to make new shapes
- explore and find perimeter, area, and volume
- use coordinate geometry to specify location and spatial relationships
- determine symmetry and congruence
- predict and explore geometric transformations such as flips, turns, and slides.
- estimate, measure, compare, and order using nonstandard and standard units of linear measurements and volume
- select appropriate tools and units of measurement

Part 1: Geometry

Materials

For each student:
- Letter #1 (p. 32)
- math journal/notebook
- pencil

Teaching Tip

Shape Word Wall

As students engage in the next lesson, a good deal of vocabulary will emerge. Record this geometry vocabulary on a word wall, bulletin board, or large chart. This word wall should contain a clear picture of each shape or geometric term as well as its name. You may want to assign pairs of students to draw and label certain shapes for the chart. This will be a classroom reference that can continually be expanded. As shapes are added to the class chart, have students add them to a chart of their own in their math journals. Include these words:

shape	rectangle
quadrilateral	hexagon
polygon	octagon
plane	trapezoid
triangle	rhombus
circle	figure
closed	kite
oval	

Super Space Stations, Inc.
(INTRODUCING SUPER SPACE STATIONS, INC.)

> **Overview:** The letter introduced in this lesson will help engage your students immediately as the fictitious Super Space Stations, Inc. asks them to help with the designing of a new space station for astronauts to use during voyages in space.

Before class starts, place copies of the letter from Super Space Stations, Inc. in a large envelope addressed to the class. (Add a return address and postage if you'd like! For added fun, have a colleague deliver the envelope to your classroom.)

Hold up the envelope and have students predict what might be inside. Open the envelope and say, "There are copies of a letter in here, and it looks like there are enough for each of us to have one. Let's pass them out so that we can all have a chance to read them."

Pass out the copies and give the class a few minutes to read the letters independently. Say, "This letter seems important. Let's read and review it together." Invite students to take turns reading the letter aloud. Lead a discussion about the letter, making sure to clarify the ideas and define any unfamiliar vocabulary. Point out the necessity of math, particularly geometry and measurement. Take the remainder of this lesson time to help students prepare individual math journals for the Space Station tasks ahead.

Literature Link

The Greedy Triangle by Marilyn Burns (Scholastic, 1995)

Readers learn about geometric shapes in this colorful, mathematical fable. A triangle is bored with his life and visits the magical shapeshifter to try and add some excitement. The shapeshifter helps to change the triangle into many different shapes before the triangle finally realizes his own worth and beauty. Geometric vocabulary is introduced and Marilyn Burns does an excellent job of portraying how the different 2-D shapes are used in our world.

ACTIVITY LESSON #2

Alien Sort

(*Investigating 2-Dimensional Shapes*)

Overview: Doing a sort with shapes helps students focus on the attributes of shapes and so begin to develop good definitions of various shapes and geometry terms.

Partner up students. Prepare the "alien cards" beforehand by having a set cut out for each partner group. If this is not possible, begin the lesson by having partners quickly cut out their cards and leave them at one partner's desk before meeting together as a class.

Say, "Today's activity will help get you ready for your upcoming challenge from Super Space Stations. You have been given a set of alien cards. Your job today is to sort these cards into groups and label each group with a sorting rule that explains the reason they have been grouped together. To do this, we should look carefully at the shapes used to create the aliens."

Model for the students by holding up Set A of the teacher's cards. (*Set A contains aliens with the same face shape in common.*) Ask, "If I were to sort these cards together in a group, what label could I give it to explain its sorting rule? Remember to look carefully at the shapes used to create the alien." (*They all have square faces.*)

Next, hold up Set B of the teacher's cards and follow the same procedure. (*Set B contains aliens with diamond-shaped, or rhombus-shaped, eyes.*)

Explain, "Face shape and eye shape are only a couple of the ways these aliens can be sorted. There is usually more than one right sorting rule. As long as you can explain your sorting rule, and show how it applies for each card, you will be correct."

Have students get their cards and begin. The sorting should take approximately 20–30 minutes.

End by allowing each pair to share one of its sorting methods. As you work through this final step, discuss shape vocabulary that emerges. This will give you an opportunity to assess some of what students know about the basic 2-D shapes. A more in-depth look at shape vocabulary is the focus of the next lesson.

Materials

For each student:
- Practice Page #2 (p. 35)
- Review Page #2 (p. 36)
- pencil

For each pair of students:
- set of Alien Cards (p. 34)
- scissors

For teacher:
- Card Sets A and B (p. 33)

Teaching Tip

Shape Sort Mysteries

Doing more sorts with students is a good idea. Sorts really focus students on the attributes of shapes and thus their defining characteristics. You can provide partners with a set of pattern blocks and ask them to create groups of shapes and identify a sorting rule that the rest of the class must try to guess. You can also set up sorts of your own at several stations around the room and have students move from station to station recording what they think your "mystery sort rule" is for each grouping.

Materials

For each student:

• 2-D Shape Handbook page (p. 37)

• geoboard

• rubber band

• Polygons Reference Chart (p. 38)

• Quadrilaterals Reference Chart (p. 39)

• math journal/notebook

• pencil

• Practice Page #3 (p. 40)

• Review Page #3 (p. 41)

Literature Link

The Silly Story of Goldie Locks and the Three Squares by Grace Maccarone (Scholastic, 1996)

Goldie Locks, the great-great-granddaughter of the original Goldilocks, enters a strange house and discovers geometric shapes. This is an entertaining, mathematical twist on a familiar fairy tale. Lots to laugh about and learn.

ACTIVITY LESSON #3

Shapes in Space

(IDENTIFYING 2-DIMENSIONAL SHAPES AND THEIR ATTRIBUTES)

Overview: This lesson focuses on describing the attributes of the most common 2-dimensional shapes. Students will be looking at sides, corners (angles), length of lines, straight or curved lines, parallel and perpendicular lines. Plan on spending two to three class periods to complete.

Explain to students, "Today you will begin your first task from Super Space Stations. You are going to help the alien architects design windows for the new space station."

Say, "Super Space Stations, Inc. has hired a team of alien architects to work on the new station and to make it as comfortable and useful to Earth astronauts as possible. However, the architects are unfamiliar with our common shapes and their attributes. Attributes are features that describe how a shape looks; for example, how many sides or corners it has. Our job is to create a handbook to help the alien architects learn about our shapes. This will help them design the windows properly."

Continue, "Before we actually begin the handbook however, let's take a look around our environment and see what shapes are used in our Earth buildings." Partner students up and give them a blank piece of paper and a pencil. "I would like you to take the next ten minutes to go on a shape hunt throughout our room (or school). Write down all the shapes you see and note where you see them. For example, I noticed our door is a rectangle, so on my paper I would write *door/ rectangle.*"

Have students do the shape hunt and then come together as a class again to share back what they noticed. Begin to work toward the idea of defining shapes by their attributes. For example if a student says, "We noticed the coat rack has a triangle shape," ask, "What is a triangle?" Have students try to define the shape idea. Continue to extend their definition by asking questions. If a student says, "A triangle has three sides," ask, "Are they all straight? Are they connected? Are they all the same size?" Do one or two shapes as examples to get students thinking about these ideas.

Hold up a copy of 2-D Shape Handbook page and say, "It's good that you noticed how we use shapes to create our buildings, furniture, and other items. Now we can use this information to help us create the handbook. This is what a blank page from the handbook looks like.

Let's complete this page together as an example. On each page you will need to include the name of the shape, a drawing of the shape, and a list of the attributes of the shape." Do a page for the triangle together. Have students build a triangle on their geoboards and record attributes they notice, such as polygon, closed, three sides, and three corners. Have them share these ideas and complete a class example page on the overhead.

Explain, "You must include the following shapes in your handbook: square, rectangle, circle, and triangle. If you have time, please add other shapes that interest you. Always build each shape first on your geoboard before you draw it."

Once students have completed their work independently, gather as a group to share and compare pages on each shape. This is a good time to add a list of attributes to the shapes on your shape word wall. Now each shape will not only have a picture and a name, but also attributes that create a definition. You may also wish to include some of the new attribute vocabulary such as sides, angles, and corners. Have students add this to their math journals as well.

Literature Link

The Shape Of Me and Other Stuff by Dr. Seuss (Random House, 1973 and 1997)

Use this book to encourage your students to think about shapes that they may have never considered before. Students are taken beyond circles, triangles, and squares, and challenged to ponder the shape of camels, beans, mice, big machines, and more. Illustrations are done in silhouette to draw attention to the outlines of figures.

Teaching Tip

Keeping Those Shapes Straight

As students find shapes on their shape hunt and add them to their handbooks, a variety of names and terms will emerge. The information below can be helpful in keeping these ideas organized.

Polygons
Most shapes we will encounter here are polygons. A polygon is a closed figure whose sides are all line segments. The name of a polygon is determined by the number of sides it has. These are common polygons:

triangle: 3 sides
quadrilateral: 4 sides
pentagon: 5 sides
hexagon: 6 sides
octagon: 8 sides

Use a copy of the Polygons Reference Chart on p. 38 to help students learn about these shapes.

Quadrilaterals
A quadrilateral is a polygon with 4 sides. There are quite a few quadrilaterals with some overlap among the terms.

Here are the most common:

parallelogram: a quadrilateral that has opposite sides the same length and parallel

rhombus: a quadrilateral where all four sides (both pairs) are the same length and parallel (A square and a diamond are also rhombuses.)

rectangle: a quadrilateral that has four right angles or square corners

square: a type of rhombus with all sides the same length

trapezoid: a polygon that has one pair of parallel sides

kite: a polygon that has two pairs of adjacent sides that are equal in length, with no sides that are parallel.

Use the Quadrilaterals Reference Chart on p. 39 to help students understand these shapes and their relationships.

Materials

For each student:
- Practice Page #4 (p. 43)
- Review Page #4 (p. 44)
- pencil

For each student pair:
- 2 copies of the Shape Memory Cards (p. 42)
- scissors

Teaching Tip

Why Work in Pairs?

Partners working together on math can be a very advantageous arrangement for everyone. Partnerships foster a supportive, safe learning situation for each student. It also provides students an opportunity to verbalize and discuss what they are learning, which helps to solidify concepts and skills. Struggling students receive support from peers, while more capable students solidify their knowledge by "teaching" a peer. Always require *both* partners to record the work and answers on individual sheets and be prepared to explain all work.

ACTIVITY LESSON #4

Shape Memory Game
(RECOGNIZING SIMILAR AND CONGRUENT SHAPES)

Overview: Students begin to explore similarity and congruence using a simple card game.

Tell the class, "Today we will be playing a memory game that will help us compare 2-D shapes. To play, we must know two important geometry words; *congruent* and *similar*. Figures that are the exact same shape and size are called "congruent." Figures that are the same shape, but *not* the same size are called "similar." The object of this game will be to find two cards that have similar or congruent shapes."

congruent   similar

   Show an example on chart paper of figures that are the same shape but not congruent and figures that are congruent. Then draw four more pairs of figures and ask the students to identify if they are the same shape or if they are congruent.

   Explain, "With your partner you will cut out two copies of the Shape Memory Cards sheet. Mix the cards together and lay them out in six rows of six. Take turns flipping over two cards and looking at the figures. If they are similar or congruent shapes, identify them that way and keep them as a match. If you forget, your partner may take the pair from you. Continue to flip two cards at a time until you are unable to make a match. The object of the game is to collect as many pairs as possible. The player with the most pairs at the end is the memory game winner."

   Pair up students and pass out scissors and two copies of the Shape Memory Cards (p. 42).

   Circulate as students play. Review their matched pairs and ask for justification to make sure that all students understand the difference between similar and congruent shapes.

ACTIVITY LESSON #5

Putting Together/Taking Apart Shapes

(RECOGNIZING SHAPES WITHIN OTHER SHAPES)

Overview: Students investigate how some shapes are composed of other common shapes.

Say, "The aliens have been working hard on the new Space Station. The other day they were asked to create some decorative artwork for the main meeting area. The aliens had created six different displays out of large pieces of tile, but during transportation to the space station they were dropped and broken. Fortunately, the displays were in separate crates so the aliens know which pieces go with which design. Luckily, the displays broke into perfect, smaller shapes."

Say, "Look at this shape. (Place a rhombus pattern block on the overhead.) What other shapes could be put together to make this?" Place one example of each pattern block across the bottom of the overhead. Ask a volunteer to share a possible solution by building the shape on the overhead using pattern blocks. (*2 triangles*) Repeat this process with a trapezoid. If students do not realize that there is more than one way to create the trapezoid using the other pattern blocks, guide them to it by saying, "What other pieces could we use to create this shape?" (*1 square and 2 triangles or 1 rhombus and 1 triangle*)

Explain, "Your job is to help the aliens rebuild the decorative artwork for the meeting area. You will be given a copy of the Master Shapes sheets that show the outlines of the original designs. Use your pattern blocks to rebuild these designs using smaller pieces. After you fill a shape, slide the pieces off piece by piece while tracing, in order to give the aliens a plan to work from."

Place a copy of the first Master Shape Sheet on the overhead. Ask a volunteer to come up and cover the design using the pattern blocks. Demonstrate for students how to slide one shape off at a time while tracing around the edges. Then pass out a copy of Master Shapes 1 to each student. While students work, help them with tracing and finding various solutions as necessary. After completion, share solutions for one of the designs using your overhead copy. (Students who finish Master Shapes 1 can try Master Shapes 2.) Finally collect all the solutions and explain that the work will be sent to the aliens so that they can fix their artwork and complete their decorating task.

Materials

For each student:
- Master Shapes 1 (p. 46)
- Master Shapes 2 (p. 47)
- Practice Page #5 (p. 48)
- Review Page #5 (p. 49)
- pencil

For teacher:
- class set of pattern blocks *
- overhead pattern blocks
- Transparency of Master Shapes 1
- overhead marker

*Note: If pattern blocks are not available, use multiple copies of Pattern Blocks (p. 45) on heavy stock paper to create your own.

Literature Link

Grandfather Tang's Story by Ann Tompert (Bantam Doubleday Dell, 1997)

Grandfather Tang and his granddaughter, Little Soo, tell a tale about two competitive fox fairies who can change their shape. The pair use a traditional Chinese puzzle, a tangram, to help tell the story. The seven pieces of the tangram are continuously shifted and arranged into different patterns.

Materials

- Practice Page #6 (p. 51)
- Review Page #6 (p. 52)
- pencil

For each pair of students:
- math journals/notebooks
- set of 3-D shapes
- 3-D Journal Shapes (p. 50)
- glue stick
- scissors

Literature Link

Sir Cumference and the Sword in the Cone: A Math Adventure by Cindy Neuschwander (Charlesbridge, 2003)

In this math-oriented mystery, Sir Cumference, Radius, and Sir Vertex search for Edgecalibur, the sword that King Arthur has hidden in a geometric solid. This mathematical journey takes the hero, Vertex, through several geometric challenges in his quest to find Edgecalibur and become King Arthur's heir, while readers learn all about 3-D shapes along the way.

ACTIVITY LESSON #6

3-D Shape Sort

(INVESTIGATING 3-DIMENSIONAL SHAPES)

> Overview: Three-dimensional solids/shapes that will be explored in this lesson include: sphere, cube, square pyramid, rectangular prism, triangular prism, cone, and cylinder.

Say, "Today you have been given a set of 3-D shapes. We say they are 3-D, or three-dimensional, because they have three dimensions: length, width, and height. Shapes that are 2-D have only two dimensions: length and width. You must sort these 3-D shapes into different groups following a sorting rule that you decide on. You need to be able to explain your sorting rule and make sure it applies to each shape in your groups. This activity will help you prepare for your upcoming challenges from Super Space Stations."

Model for the students by holding up a pyramid and a cube. Ask, "If I were to sort these together in a group, what label could I give it to explain its sorting rule?" (*Each has a square face.*)

Next, hold up a pyramid and a triangular prism and repeat the question above. (*These two shapes both have faces that are triangular.*)

This would be a good time to introduce and explain the terms *face*, *corner*, and *edge*. A face is one of the flat surfaces around a 3-D shape. Corners are the points where several faces meet and an edge is where two faces meet. Use the cube to demonstrate what these definitions mean. (*It would be helpful to also include these on the picture word wall.*)

Explain to the students they should consider a variety of different ways to sort and classify these shapes. Encourage them to be creative and to find new ways or more than one way to sort. Remind them that they are responsible for explaining their sorting rule and showing how it applies to each item in their set.

Say, "To record your sorts, cut out the 3-D journal shapes and paste them into your journals. Write the corresponding sorting rule on the other side of the same page. Send students back to their work stations to begin the activity in pairs. Circulate as students work, supplying vocabulary, asking questions, and encouraging students to verbalize their thinking.

Students should need approximately 30 minutes to work at sorting and classifying the 3-D shapes.

End with a group discussion. Allow each group to share one of its sorting methods. You may wish to ask students if there are any remaining geoblocks that they had trouble identifying and naming.

. . . .

ACTIVITY LESSON #7

3-D Space Buttons

(*IDENTIFYING 3-DIMENSIONAL SHAPES AND THEIR ATTRIBUTES*)

Overview: If possible, use the Literature Link, *Captain Invincible and the Space Shapes*, to introduce the 3-D shapes in this lesson.

Say, "Today we are going to look carefully at three dimensional or 3-D shapes. The aliens are designing a control panel that will have buttons with a variety of 3-D shapes." Show the overhead copy of the 3-D Space Buttons Sheet. The first shape listed is a cube. Say, "Pick up a cube from your 3-D shape set and examine it closely. How many faces does it have? Remember, faces are the flat surfaces." (*6*) Model how to record the six faces on the chart. Move onto corners, reminding students that corners are the points where several faces meet. (*8*) Model how to record the corners. Move onto edges, reminding students that edges are the lines where two faces meet. (*12*) Model how to record the edges on the chart.

Explain, "This last column is for you to use your creativity and come up with an idea for what the cube-shaped button on the control panel will do. Try to think of an idea that would be useful for the space station, yet is also related to the shape of the button. For example, the cube-shaped button could be pressed to produce ice cubes. Does anyone have another idea?" (Allow several students to share ideas. If you read *Captain Invincible and the Space Shapes*, refer back to it and see if students remember how the cube was used in the story.)

Distribute 3-D Space Buttons sheets and have students begin. As you circulate, check to make sure that students are physically handling the 3-D shapes to determine the number of faces, corners, and edges before recording. Ask students to "verify" some of their answers by demonstrating for you with the 3-D shapes.

Materials

. . . .

For each student:
- 3-D Space Buttons (p. 53)
- set of 3-D shapes, including sphere, cube, pyramid, rectangular prism, triangular prism, cone, and cylinder *
- pencil
- Practice Page #7 (p. 54)
- Review Page #7 (p. 55)

*Note: Students may share, but they will need to observe and handle each shape independently.

For teacher:
- Transparency of 3-D Space Buttons
- overhead marker

Literature Link

. . . .

Captain Invincible and the Space Shapes by Stuart J. Murphy (HarperCollins, 2001)

This book is an excellent tool for introducing the attributes of 3-D shapes. The comic book layout provides information about common geometric shapes. Captain Invincible and his space dog, Comet, use their knowledge of 3-D shapes, including cubes, cones, and pyramids, to help them navigate past many obstacles. Will they make it home safely?

Materials

For each student:
- Practice Page #8 (p. 57)
- Review Page #8 (p. 58)
- pencil

For each student pair:
- square inch graph paper
- a supply of square pattern blocks
- crayons or markers

For Teacher:
- Symmetrical Shapes sheet (p. 56), cut apart into individual shapes, enough so that each student gets a shape *
- Transparency of square inch graph paper
- overhead square pattern blocks

*Note: Several students will have the same shape.

Literature Link

Let's Fly a Kite by Stuart J. Murphy (HarperCollins, 2000)

This book works well to start or supplement your lesson on mirror symmetry. Two siblings argue over everything during their day at the beach. Illustrations nicely depict the method used to divide everyday objects into two identical halves or parts. Examples of nonsymmetry are shown as well, adding to the understanding of the concept.

ACTIVITY LESSON #8

Fabulous Flags
(MIRROR SYMMETRY)

Overview: Students explore mirror symmetry and investigate shapes with more than one line of symmetry.

Tell the class, "Today you will be designing a flag for the super space station. Super Space Stations, Inc. has asked that the flag have mirror symmetry. Shapes that can be flipped or folded over a line so that one half is on top of the other half have mirror symmetry. The two halves are mirror images of each other."

unfolded   folded   unfolded   folded

Say, "Let's start with an activity that focuses on mirror symmetry." Explain, "You will be given a shape, like this oval (hold up provided "teacher shape" for students). You will need to first cut it out and then try folding it to find a line of symmetry. You will know that you have found a line of symmetry if both sides are equal in shape and size, or congruent." Model how to cut out and fold the oval, displaying the line of symmetry you have created. Folding the shape along the line of symmetry will prove to the students that it has mirror symmetry.

Pass out the shapes so that each student gets one. Give the students five minutes to cut out, explore, and fold the shapes. Then gather the class, asking students to bring their shapes with them. Start with the simpler shapes, such as the square and rectangle. Ask all students with the same shape to stand and demonstrate how they folded it. Point out when children have folded the same shape in different ways, finding different lines of symmetry. Discuss how some shapes can have more than one line of symmetry. Work through all of the shapes, asking if there is more than one line of symmetry.

Say, "Now you are ready to work with a partner and create a flag with mirror symmetry." Hold up the square-inch graph paper, explaining that it will be the template for the flag.

Explain, "Your first job is to fold the paper showing a line of symmetry. You will need to agree with your partner on which line to use before folding the paper." (Model one way of folding the paper for the students.)

Place your overhead copy of the square-inch graph paper on the projector. Draw the line of symmetry you have chosen. "Next, you will use square pattern blocks to fill one side of your paper with a design that both partners like." (Model how to begin doing this on the overhead.)

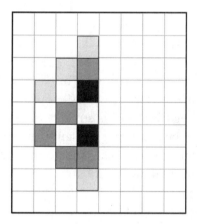 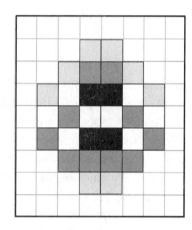

Explain, "On the other side of the paper, you will then use the pattern block squares to create a mirror image of your original design. (Model this.) If you complete this job correctly, both halves of your paper should look the same. At this point, you need to check with me. Once I okay the design, replace the blocks with coloring. One partner will work on each side of the flag. Together you will remove the same block on each of the sides, decide upon a color for that shape, and fill in the space on the paper. You should continue working in this way until the entire flag is complete. Remember, your side must exactly match your partner's side in shapes and colors." (Ask a student to be your partner and model this procedure for the class).

As students set to work, circulate to make sure that they are working together and creating flags with mirror symmetry.

Materials

For each student:

- Martian Mix-Up (p. 59)
- pencil
- Practice Page #9 (p. 60)
- Review Page #9 (p. 61)

For teacher:

- class set of pattern blocks
- overhead pattern blocks
- Transparency of Martian Mix-Up
- overhead marker

Teaching Tip

Defining Flips, Slides, and Turns

Students need to understand that the terms "flip," "slide," and "turn" are useful when describing how a shape has been moved or transformed. A "flip" can also be called a "reflection," because a shape or object is reflected over an imaginary line. A "flip" is the movement of a shape from front to back, top to bottom, or bottom to top without turning. Flips may be horizontal or vertical. A "slide" is also called a "translation" and describes the movement of a shape right, left, up, or down without changing sides or rotating. It is similar to a "push" in one direction. A "turn" is also called a "rotation." It is the rotating of a shape around a single point without flipping.

ACTIVITY LESSON #9

Martian Mix-Up
(FLIPS, SLIDES, AND TURNS)

> Overview: A look at how 2-D shapes can be moved on a plane through flips, slides, and turns.

Place a trapezoid pattern block on the left-hand corner of your overhead projector. Place another one in the right-hand corner and then turn your projector on. Ask, "If this trapezoid started here and ended up here, what happened to it?" (*It slid.*)

Say, "Close your eyes and try to picture in your mind how the shape was moved." (By asking students to visualize what happened to the original shape, you are providing them with a strategy to use later when working independently.) Have students explain their answers and physically show you what happened, using the overhead. Explain, "To slide a shape means to move it along in any direction without turning it."

Turn off the overhead. Place a trapezoid in the center of the projector. Then flip a second trapezoid to sit above it.

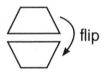

Turn your projector on and ask, "If this trapezoid started here and ended up here, what happened to it?" (*It flipped.*) Follow the procedure above to demonstrate. Explain, "To flip a shape is to reflect it over a line." Put the trapezoid back in its original position, draw a line by its right side, then flip it over the line you have drawn to reinforce this idea.

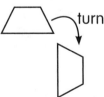

Turn the projector off for the last time. Place a trapezoid horizontally in the center of the projector. Turn a second trapezoid vertically to the right of it. Turn the projector on and ask "If this trapezoid started here and ended up here, what happened to it?" (*It turned.*) Follow the procedure above to demonstrate. Explain, "To turn a shape is to rotate it around a point." Put the trapezoid back in its original position, draw a dot by the right lower corner, then turn/ rotate the trapezoid around the point to reinforce this idea. Explain, "Slides, flips, and turns change the position of shapes, but they do not change their form or size."

Explain, "Today we have a problem to solve for Super Space Stations, Inc. The alien workers laid out a tile design for the floor in the control room of the new space station. They worked all day to plan the design. That night, Marty the Martian decided to play one of his famous practical jokes. He snuck into the space station and slid, flipped, and turned some of the tiles in the design. This is quite a 'Martian Mix-Up!' The alien workers are very upset because they really worked hard and were proud of their original design. They need your help to put the tiles back. You will need to figure out if the mixed-up tiles were slid, flipped, or turned."

Place the overhead copy of the Martian Mix-Up Sheet (p. 59) on the projector. Say, "Super Space Stations, Inc. sent us a copy of the mixed-up tiles. You will need to look at each tile and decide whether it shows a slide, flip, or turn. Once you have determined which of the three it is by moving your pattern blocks to prove your answer, you need to write "slide," "flip," or "turn" in the space provided. Let's try one together."

Examine the first example with the students. Give them time to visualize and predict a slide, flip, or turn. Have a volunteer demonstrate the correct answer by manipulating a pattern block on the overhead. Model how to write the answer on the line. Say, "Now it is your turn to finish this job. Remember that you must use pattern blocks to prove your answer before writing it on the line, like we just did. Also, remember to try and use visualizing as a strategy to help you see how the piece was moved." As students work, circulate to ensure that they are actually moving the pattern blocks to verify their answers.

Teaching Tips

Body Geometry

An excellent way to give students experience with "flips," "slides," and "turns" is to have them use their own bodies to demonstrate the movements. Have students lie on the floor on their backs or stomachs and ask them to show you a flip. They should move from their backs to their stomachs, their stomachs to their backs. They may also "flip" feet to head. Next have students demonstrate a slide, beginning on either their backs or stomachs. Make sure students note that the direction of their feet does not change. Finally have students demonstrate a "turn" starting on their side. They can use their shoulder as a point of rotation. Actually experiencing each move will provide a clearer understanding for your students.

Icy Slides, Flips and Turns

This Web site by Harcourt School Publishers is great for a whole-class demonstration. It shows the movements of flips, slides, and turns through animation and the use of pattern blocks. After a whole-class introduction, students can play the game individually for added practice. http://www.harcourtschool.com/activity/icy_slides_flips_turns/

Materials

For each student:
- 2 sheets of paper *
- crayons/colored pencils
- Practice Page #10 (p. 62)
- Review Page #10 (p. 63)
- pencil

* Note: You may provide these "radical rotation" sheets with a dot already drawn in the middle of the page, or have students do this simple step themselves.

For teacher:
- set of overhead (or regular) pattern blocks
- Transparency with a dot drawn in the middle of the page
- overhead marker
- class set of pattern blocks

ACTIVITY LESSON #10

Radical Rotations
(ROTATIONAL SYMMETRY)

> Overview: Students explore rotational symmetry, completing existing designs and creating their own.

Put the transparency with the dot on the overhead. (You may want to refer to this as a "radical rotation" sheet.) Place three triangle pattern blocks in a rotating pattern at the center dot.

Turn the projector on. Point to the first triangle and ask, "If the first triangle was placed here, and the second and third triangles were placed like this, where would the fourth triangle need to go in order to continue this rotating pattern?" Have a volunteer come up and demonstrate. Once the fourth triangle is correctly placed, explain, "These triangles are showing a different kind of symmetry called rotational symmetry. The same shape is rotating, or moving in a circle, around a central point until meeting up with the starting shape." Ask volunteers to come up and help you complete the design in order to completely demonstrate the rotational symmetry.

Say, "The alien workers at the new space station finished the tile floor in the control room, thanks to your help. They have now started a new project. They are tiling the floor of the main entrance to the space station. This floor will have two designs on it. The alien workers have begun the first design, but they were confused by the rotational symmetry and need your help to finish it. They also need you to create the second design using rotational symmetry and your creativity!"

Show the transparency of a "radical rotation" sheet. Be sure that students have pattern blocks and their own copy of a radical rotation sheet so that they can work along at their desks. Say, "This is what the workers have completed so far. They began the design with two rhombuses." Ask a volunteer to come up and place two pattern blocks on top of their spots on the sheet. Tell students to do the same at their desks. Next ask, "How should we place the next rhombus to continue the rotational symmetry in this design? Give it a try." Model the correct placement for the students. Next, demonstrate how to trace the pattern block using your overhead marker, tracing only the outer sides that were not already shown. Tell students to do the same on their papers.

Explain, "You need to complete the rest of the design this way, placing one block at a time, tracing it, and then moving on. The design will be complete once you rotate around the circle and come back to the starting shape."

Continue, "Once you complete this design, you have a second design to create on your own. Remember to first find the center point that your design will rotate around. You need to choose one pattern block shape to begin your design. Once it is placed, remember to trace the first shape completely. When the other shapes are placed, you will only need to trace the outer sides. Once both designs are finished you should color them. I will collect your work and send it to the alien workers so that they can complete the floor."

Circulate and observe how students are using the manipulatives and tracing each block as they work. If students have difficulty tracing, suggest that they ask a partner to hold the block for them as they trace around it.

Teaching Tip

Organizing Materials

Organizing materials ahead of time so that students can get to them quickly and easily will help math lessons that use manipulatives run smoothly. Purchase large plastic baskets from a dollar store to use as "math baskets." If your class is arranged into table groups, be sure to have one basket per table group. Otherwise, have enough baskets so that 5–6 children can share one. Place enough materials for the groups in the math baskets before the lessons. Place baskets in a centralized location so that group members can access the materials as they need them. This will help prevent disruptions as students look for materials or wait for supplies to be passed out to them. It is also more efficient than having students keep the materials in their desks.

Materials

For each student:

• Luxury Lounge Floor Plan (p. 64)

• Lounging Around Coordinates
  (p. 65)

• Practice Page #11 (p. 66)

• Review Page #11 (p. 67)

• pencil

For teacher:

• Transparency of Luxury Lounge
  Floor Plan

• 15 one-inch squares, cubes, or
  counters (to place on the overhead
  for modeling)

ACTIVITY LESSON #11

Lounging Around

(COORDINATE GRIDS)

> Overview: In this lesson students will practice finding and naming points on a coordinate grid with ordered pairs.

Place 15 overhead manipulatives, such as one-inch squares, on the overhead in three rows, with five in each row:

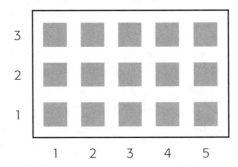

Ask the students, "How many squares are in each row?" *(5)* "How many rows are there?" *(3)*

Label the coordinates as shown in the illustration as the students watch. As you label, explain that you are creating a coordinate grid. Say, "A coordinate grid is a graph used to locate points."

Touch the third square in the second row. Ask the students, "Which row is this square in?" *(Row 2)* Ask, "Looking at the second row, which position is this square in?" *(third)* Continue, "This is the third square in the second row."

Say, "There is an easier way to name the location of this square. You can use ordered pairs to name locations on a coordinate grid. These rows and columns form lines that go across and up and down. When the lines cross, or intersect, they form a specific point or ordered pair. The first number in the ordered pair is how many spaces you move to the right." Circle the square on the overhead and ask, "How many spaces do you move to the right, or along the bottom of the grid?" *(3)* Continue, "So the first number in my ordered pair would be 3 and I would write it like this: (3, __)." (Be sure to say "parentheses, three, comma, space for the next number, parentheses.")

"The next number in the ordered pair is how many spaces you move up. How many spaces do you move up the grid? You can use the numbers along the side of the grid to help you." (2)

Continue, "So the second number in my ordered pair would be 2, and I would write it like this: (3, 2)."

Explain, "When I move my finger across three and I move my other finger up 2, the place where they cross is the location of our inch square: (3, 2)." Try several more examples with the class, asking volunteers to name and write the coordinates.

Place the transparency of the Luxury Lounge Floor Plan on the overhead. Say, "Space Stations, Inc. needs our help designing a luxury lounge for their new space station. This lounge will be a place for astronauts to relax and have fun. They have sent us a floor plan of the lounge. Like many floor plans, it is a coordinate grid. Ten locations have been marked at points where the lines on the grid intersect. We have also been sent a list of ten objects that need to be arranged in the new lounge. Your task is to place the objects in appropriate locations and record their positions."

Pass out a copy of the Lounging Around Coordinates sheet to each student. Have them silently read the directions at the top of the page.

Say, "The first object we need to place is an air hockey table, where do you think we should put it?" Have a volunteer come up and label the location "air hockey table" in the appropriate rectangle on the floor plan. Ask the student to explain his or her reasons for placing the object in the chosen location.

Say, "Now that we have chosen a location for the air hockey table, we need to fill in its ordered pair on the Lounging Around Coordinates sheet. Ask another volunteer to name the location of the air hockey table. Have all students write the ordered pair on their papers.

Tell students, "Complete the rest of this task on your own. After you have placed all ten items, use your creativity to decide on four more objects for the lounge and place them on the floor plan as well. Place each object according to the ordered pairs listed on the chart."

As students begin work, ensure that they are following all steps and writing ordered pairs in the correct order. Reversing the order of coordinates is a common error. To help students remember that the horizontal axis is written first and then the vertical, remind them that "in the morning, you are lying down before you get up."

Teaching Tip

They're Not, They Are, Which Are?

Continue to help students review geometry terms by playing "They're Not, They Are, Which Are?" Begin by choosing a term like *quadrilateral*. Draw three large boxes on the board or on a paper. Label the first box, "They're Not." In that box draw some figures that are not quadrilaterals. Label the next box, "They are," and draw some quadrilaterals. Label the last box, "Which Are?" and draw several figures, some of which are quadrilaterals and some which are not. Have students try to figure out which figures or terms are the correct ones in the last box by studying the information provided in the first box. Play this game with lots of different geometry concepts. Students can even make up their own to test each other.

Part 2: Measurement

Materials

For each student:
- Letter #12 (p. 68)
- Measurement Recording Sheet (p. 69)
- pencil
- Practice Page #12 (p. 70)
- Review Page #12 (p. 71)

For teacher:
- class set of pattern blocks
- overhead pattern blocks
- Transparency of Measurement Recording Sheet
- overhead marker

Literature Link

How Big Is a Foot? by Rolf Myller (Bantam Doubleday Dell, 1991)

This fable cleverly shows the need for standard measurement. The King wants to give the Queen a bed as a birthday present. The trouble is that no one in the kingdom knows the answer to a very important question: How big is a bed? The King uses his feet to measure, and gives the measurements to his apprentice. When the apprentice makes the bed, he uses his own tiny feet to measure, and the bed is too small for the queen. How can this problem be solved? Standard measurement!

ACTIVITY LESSON #12

Measuring Up
(NONSTANDARD MEASUREMENT)

Overview: This lesson focuses on the concept of measurement and nonstandard measures before examining specific measurement units.

Distribute copies of Letter #12 to students. (See the procedure suggested in Activity Lesson #1.) After students have read the letter and you have reviewed it as a class, say, "I have been informed that Super Space Stations, Inc. is planning to build a teaching classroom lab. It will be used for visitors to learn about space and the solar system. Your job will be to measure various items around our classroom so that they can use our measurements to build these same items in their space station."

Explain, "The alien workers are not familiar with our units of standard measurement so they will be using the "Space Units" (pattern blocks) sent down to us from Super Space Stations, Inc."

Pair up students and pass out a Measurement Recording Sheet to each student. Distribute pattern blocks to all groups. Identify all the classroom objects students will need to measure around the room. Point out where they will be recording the number of "Space Units" they use to measure each item.

Teaching Tip

Measurement Chart

As you work with your students on learning about measurement, you may want to keep a vocabulary chart. Charting vocabulary as you cover it reinforces student understanding and provides assistance when students are explaining their thinking orally or in writing. Students should also copy vocabulary into their own math journals along with an example to show their understanding. Include terms such as these:

nonstandard	inch	area
standard	foot	perimeter
U.S. Customary	yard	volume
metric	millimeter	length
ruler	centimeter	width
yardstick	meter	height

Say, "When you measure, label your answer so that it is clear which unit of measure was used." Show the students how the recording sheet has the label "Space Units" written after the second line.

Explain that the students will need to choose the specific unit that will make the measuring most efficient. Point out that if it is a big item, they may want to use the biggest space unit, and if it is smaller, they may choose a unit that is more appropriate.

Ask a volunteer to read the first item to be measured. Discuss which Space Unit would be most appropriate to use when measuring a classroom doorknob. Ask the students to explain why it is the best unit for the job. Before measuring, have students estimate the measurement in the chosen units. Estimating before actually measuring helps students build measurement number sense.

Now have the pair of students use the designated unit to measure the doorknob. Be sure to explain that they must start at the edge when measuring and try to be as accurate as possible. Use the overhead copy to show students how to record the estimate, then the actual measurement and type of space units used. For example, four trapezoid space units.

As students are working, it may be necessary to address ideas like half-units if the item can not be measured exactly. Check for good measuring technique and appropriate unit choices.

ACTIVITY LESSON #13

Space Standards

(STANDARD UNITS, U.S. CUSTOMARY)

Overview: This lesson focuses on measuring with inches, feet, and yards.

Say, "Super Space Stations, Inc. is working hard to complete the teaching classroom lab using the measurements that we sent them. However, without some help from builders on Earth, they feel they may not complete the job on time. They have decided to hire some earthlings, but have run into a problem. When they shared the

Literature Links

Is a Blue Whale the Biggest Thing There Is? by Robert E. Wells (Albert Whitman, 1993)

This book is very helpful when introducing the concept of size, measurement, and magnitude. It illustrates the concept of big, bigger, and biggest by comparing the measurements of large things like a blue whale, a mountain, a star, and the universe.

Measuring Penny by Loreen Leedy (Henry Holt, 2000)

Lisa measures her dog with all sorts of units. The book covers nonstandard and standard units while exploring length, width, height, volume, temperature, and time.

Materials

For each student:
- Measurement Recording Sheet (p. 69)
- pencil
- ruler
- yardsticks (one for every 2–3 students if possible)
- Practice Page #13 (p. 72)
- Review Page #13 (p. 73)

For teacher:
- Transparency of Measurement Recording Sheet
- overhead marker

Teaching Tip

"Real-Life" Measurement

In order for students to appreciate the value of learning about measurement, brainstorm situations together where people need to use measurement. Some examples might include: buying a suit, altering clothing, hanging a picture, building something, or deciding if a new piece of furniture will fit in a room. Draw students' attention to merchandise that is advertised with measurements, such as big screen TVs, picture frames and furniture. "Real-life" connections make the math students are learning in the classroom even more meaningful.

Materials

For each student:

- Mixed-Up Measurement (p. 74)
- pencil
- ruler
- yardsticks (one for every 2–3 students if possible)
- Practice Page #14 (p. 75)
- Review Page #14 (p. 76)

For teacher:

- Transparency of Mixed-Up Measurement
- overhead marker

measurements, the earthling builders were unable to match up the space units with any familiar units of measure. The alien workers need us to measure the same classroom items again, using standard Earth measurements, in this case, U.S. Customary units."

Partner up students and pass out the Space Standards Recording Sheets, rulers, and yardsticks.

Take some time to explore the rulers and yardsticks. Compare inches, feet, and yards. Point out how these measurements are related. Explain to students, "As you measure you will need to choose the specific unit that will make the measuring most efficient. If it is a small item, you will probably want to use smaller units, like inches. As things get bigger you'll want to use bigger units, like feet and yards." Ask a volunteer to read the first item to be measured. (*doorknob*)

Discuss which "standard unit" would be most appropriate to use when measuring a classroom door knob. (*inches*) Ask why it is the best unit for the job. Next have a volunteer estimate the distance across the doorknob. Measure the doorknob in inches. Model starting at the edge of the item and the end of ruler. Then use the overhead copy to show how to record the estimate and the actual measurement, as well as the type of standard unit used.

Remind students that as they work, they may be asked to explain why they have chosen particular units. It may be necessary to address ideas like half-units if the item cannot be measured exactly.

ACTIVITY LESSON #14

Mixed-Up Measurement

(CONVERTING BETWEEN UNITS, U.S. CUSTOMARY)

> Overview: This lesson focuses on converting between units in the U.S. Customary System.

Say, "Marty the Martian is at it again! It seems that when he found a list of measurements his fellow workers left behind, he decided to mix them up. The measurements are all still accurate, but not recorded using the most appropriate or efficient unit of measurement."

Explain, "You will need to convert the measurements into more appropriate forms. You may use rulers and yardsticks for this. You won't be changing the measurements, just recording them in a form that is more useful and efficient."

Examine a ruler and yardstick together. Discuss how these measurements are related: 12" in a foot, 3' in a yard. Ask, "What kinds of objects might you measure in this classroom using inches? Using feet? Using yards?"

Look at the Mixed-Up Measurement sheet on the overhead. Ask a volunteer to read the first item to be converted. (*24 inches*) Ask, "Which unit do you think we should convert to? Why?" (*Feet, because it is more efficient to talk about something that is more than a foot, but less than a yard, in terms of feet.*)

Show where to record the answer on the sheet and have students complete the rest of the sheet independently. Have rulers and yardsticks easily accessible. Explain that in order to finish the task we need to make one table with the conversions to send back to Super Space Stations, Inc. Check work together at the end to create this table. At the bottom of the chart, write down the conversions from inches to feet to yards so that if Marty mixes up any more measurements, the aliens will be able to complete corrections on their own.

ACTIVITY LESSON #15

Metric Materials

(*STANDARD UNITS, METRIC SYSTEM*)

> Overview: This lesson focuses on measuring with millimeters and centimeters.

Say, "Super Space Station's latest project is to design and build a variety of space vehicles. The aliens were not able to find the parts they needed in our town, but yesterday they located some at a factory in Ontario, Canada. However, they have run into one problem. When the aliens sent the standard measurements to the factory, they were unable to fill the order because in Canada they do not measure using the U.S. Customary System. They use the metric system."

Explain to the students that their job will be to measure the life-sized drawings of each of the parts, using a metric ruler. Say, "Remember that whenever you measure, it is important to use the most efficient unit of measure."

Teaching Tip

U.S. Customary Units

Share the abbreviations for U.S. Customary units with students. U.S. Customary units use small letters and periods, like abbreviations for most units of measurement. It is not necessary to add an "s" to an abbreviation to show a plural, such as inches. It is helpful to create a chart of the units and their abbreviations, as well as symbols and equivalences, to use as a class reference.

in. = inch/inches
12 inches = 1 foot
ft. = foot/feet
3 feet = 1 yard
yd. = yard/yards
' = feet
" = inches

Materials

For each student:
- Metric Materials (p. 77)
- pencil
- metric ruler
- Practice Page #15 (p. 78)
- Review Page #15 (p. 79)

For teacher:
- Transparency of Metric Materials
- metric ruler for overhead
- overhead marker

Teaching Tip

Adding Metric Units to the Measurement Chart

Make your students aware that the abbreviations for metric units are also written with lowercase letters, but unlike U.S. Customary units, they do not have periods. You may wish to add the following abbreviations to the chart you created for U.S. Customary units.

mm = millimeters
cm = centimeters
m = meters
km = kilometers
10 mm = 1 cm
1,000 mm = 1 m
100 cm = 1 m
1,000 m = 1 km

Materials

For each student:
- Meter Space Exploration Model (p. 80)
- pencil
- student chair
- Practice Page #16 (p. 81)
- Review Page #16 (p. 82)

For each team of 6 students:
- roll of masking tape
- meter stick

For teacher:
- Transparency of Meter Space Exploration Model
- colored overhead markers

Pass out metric rulers. Encourage students to explore the units of measure and discuss how they are related to each other. On the overhead ruler, point out how there are 10 millimeters in a centimeter. Hold up a meter stick and point out how there are 100 centimeters in a meter. Have students decide which unit would be best for measuring very small parts and which would be best for measuring larger parts.

Say, "When you measure, you always need to label your answer so that it is clear which unit of measure was used." Show the students how they will be labeling their measurements with millimeters or centimeters on the recording sheet. Measure the first part on the overhead copy using the clear overhead ruler. As a class, record the measurement and unit used on the recording sheet

Remind students to start at the edge of the item and the end of the ruler when measuring, in order to be as accurate as possible. Stress that throughout the activity, students may be asked to explain why they have chosen particular units. Begin the activity. As students work, check for good, accurate measuring technique and appropriate unit choices.

ACTIVITY LESSON #16

Meter Space Exploration

(Standard Metric Units)

> **Overview:** This lesson focuses on creating a model of a space vehicle's outline while measuring with meters.

Say, "In this activity you will be creating a life-sized outline of the space vehicles that are being built at the new space station. You will do this by measuring out and creating a tape model outline of the space vehicle on the floor of our classroom. You will be working in groups of six, and in the end, all six of you must be able to fit inside the vehicle while sitting on your chairs."

Explain, "Since we are creating a life-sized model of the Super Space Stations, Inc. space vehicle, it will be necessary to use a larger metric unit than the ones we explored in the last lesson." Pass out meter sticks and give students the opportunity to explore them and make observations. Ask, "How are millimeters and centimeters related to the meter?" *(100 centimeters in a meter, 1,000 millimeters in a meter)*

Pass out the Meter Space Exploration Model Sheets and show the overhead copy. Discuss how to read the model plan and where students should begin their measuring for this task. Point out that the vehicle is made up of a combination of separate shapes that can be measured one by one. (It may help to highlight each shape in a different color using your overhead marker. You could also decide on a start point and label each section with numbers showing the order in which to complete the task.)

Say, "You will need to work as a team to measure out this vehicle. All members of the team are responsible for reading the model sheet and measuring tape lines. All members of the team need to be involved and work should be divided equally." Put students into their teams of six and send them to their work areas to begin. As they work, check measurements from time to time for accuracy.

Once students have successfully completed the task, ask them to move their chairs into the six squares in the middle of the ship. (It's fun to take a picture of the teams inside their model space vehicles for classroom display.)

ACTIVITY LESSON #17

Metric Mix-Up
(CONVERTING BETWEEN METRIC UNITS)

> Overview: This lesson focuses on converting between units in the metric system.

Say, "We just received notice from Super Space Stations, Inc. that Marty the Martian has done it once again! It seems that when he found the latest list of measurements for the space vehicles, he decided to mix them up. Just like last time, the measurements are all still accurate, but they are not recorded using the most appropriate metric units."

Explain, "You will need to convert the measurements into the more appropriate forms. You can use the metric rulers and meter sticks as well as our class measurement chart in order to determine how to convert the listed measurements into the most appropriate and efficient units."

Teaching Tips

Metric Measures

The Web site http://www.teachingmeasures.co.uk/menu.html offers materials for a large display as well as printable worksheets for students to learn more about metric measurement. There are three separate sections on length, mass, and capacity.

Keep on Estimating

As new measurement concepts are introduced, such as area and perimeter, continue to have students estimate before measuring. Remind students that an estimate is rarely exact; rather we just try to get as close as possible using our experience and knowledge. Estimation really helps students develop measurement skill and number sense.

Materials

For each student:
- Metric Mix-Up (p. 83)
- pencil
- metric ruler
- meter sticks
- Practice Page #17 (p. 84)
- Review Page #17 (p. 85)

For teacher:
- Transparency of Metric Mix-Up
- overhead marker

Literature Links

Twizzlers From Simple Shapes to Geometry by Jerry Pallotta (Scholastic, 2005)

This book provides clear examples of geometry concepts, starting with simple shapes and moving through more complex ideas like perimeter, circumference, types of lines, and area. Terms are defined and explained in easy-to-read language with a bit of humor.

How BIG are they? by Nicholas Harris (Flying Frog Publishing, 2004)

This intriguing book demonstrates measurements from less than an inch to hundreds of thousands of miles, through double-page illustrations drawn to scale. The text provides a variety of interesting facts; measurements are provided by the illustration captions.

Materials

For each student:
- Luxury Lounge: Area Directions (p. 86)
- Floor Plan (p. 87)
- pencil
- one-inch square tiles
- Practice Page #18 (p. 88)
- Review Page #18 (p. 89)

For teacher:
- Transparency of the Floor Plan
- overhead marker

Pass out the Metric Mix-Up Sheets. Briefly review the relationship between millimeters, centimeters, and meters. Ask students what kinds of objects they might measure around the classroom using the various units.

Look at the overhead copy of the Metric Mix-Up Sheet together. Be sure that rulers and meter sticks are easily accessible to the students. Complete the first example together. Ask a volunteer to read the first item to be converted, 1,020 millimeters. Ask which unit we should convert to and why. If they determine the correct conversion, 1 meter and 2 centimeters, ask them to demonstrate proof using the meter stick.

Model where to write in the 1 meter and 2 centimeters on the recording sheet. Have students complete the rest of the conversions independently. As you observe, notice which students use formulas for conversion and which use the measuring tools themselves.

After students have completed the conversions, explain that in order to finish the task we need to make one table with the conversions and send it back to Super Space Stations, Inc. At the bottom we need to write down the rules used to convert from millimeters to centimeters to meters, in case Marty mixes up more metric measurements.

ACTIVITY LESSON #18

Luxury Lounge Area

(CALCULATING AREA)

> Overview: This lesson focuses on calculating the area of different shapes.

Say, "In this lesson you will be finding the area of the different furniture items that Super Space Stations, Inc. would like to place in the Luxury Lounge. The alien workers need to know the area of each item so that they can determine if they will all fit in the lounge. Area is the measure of the inside of a flat or 2-D figure. We typically measure area in square units." Demonstrate by drawing a square and coloring in the interior area.

Pass out a copy of the Luxury Lounge: Area Directions to each student. Tell students, "You will be completing this task by finding the area of the given furniture shapes. We will use one-inch square tiles to measure the area."

Fill in the first shape, the bookcase, on the overhead using one-inch squares. After filling the shape, slide off one tile at a time while counting. Once the total number is discovered, explain that the answer will be labeled using the unit *square inches*. *(4 square inches)*

Send students back to their desks to complete the rest of the activity independently. Circulate as students work, ensuring that they are following all the steps. This lesson contains multistep directions, which are challenging for some students. Also watch to be sure that students are remembering to label the area of each shape "square inches."

ACTIVITY LESSON #19

Perimeter Proof

(CALCULATING PERIMETER)

> Overview: This lesson focuses on calculating the perimeter of different shapes.

Place the transparency of the Floor Plan on the overhead. Say, "In this lesson you will be using the same shapes you found in the last activity, but this time you will be finding and recording the perimeter of the different furniture items that Super Space Stations, Inc. would like to place in the Luxury Lounge."

Pass out a copy of the Luxury Lounge: Perimeter Directions and the Floor Plan to students. Have them silently read the directions page. Tell students, "Perimeter is a measure of the distance around a shape. Think of it as a fence. The sides of a shape are each measured and totaled together to give us the perimeter of the shape. We will be measuring the perimeter of these shapes in inches."

Model how to use the one-inch square tiles to help count around the perimeter of the first shape. Label each inch as you count them. Finally, write and label the perimeter under the shape. *(10 inches)* Measure with a ruler as a check and to demonstrate another way to measure perimeter.

Have students complete the rest of the activity independently. Circulate to ensure that students are following all steps.

Teaching Tip

Encouragement and Reward

At the culmination of the geometry and measurement tasks presented in this book, you may want to consider a final reward for all the students. In honor of their dedication to relearning and mastering these difficult skills, red, white, and blue "rocket" ice pops from Super Space Stations, Inc. is a nice final thank-you. When you share the Super Space Station's Thank-You Note (p. 92), with the class, you can also provide a snack.

Materials

For each student:
- Luxury Lounge: Perimeter Directions (p. 86)
- Floor Plan (p. 87)
- pencil
- one-inch square tiles
- Practice Page #19 (p. 90)
- Review Page #19 (p. 91)

For teacher:
- Transparency of the Floor Plan
- overhead ruler
- overhead marker

Super Space Stations, Inc.

Dear Students,

   Greetings! My name is Ms. Ali On. I am the president of a company called Super Space Stations, Inc. Our company builds space stations for astronauts in outer space. Astronauts land at these stations during space voyages in order to conduct experiments and do research.

   My company is about to design and build our most spectacular space station yet, and we'd like to ask for your assistance. We will need your help with designing certain components of this new station. You will need to use your best math skills and thinking. Geometry, measurement, and problem solving are needed to complete the tasks involved in this project.

   I've heard what wonderful mathematicians and thinkers you are, so I sincerely hope that you will agree to help us with our exciting space adventure.

Best Regards,

Ms. Ali On

President
Super Space Stations, Inc.

Reteaching Math: Geometry & Measurement © 2008 by Bob Krech, Scholastic Teaching Resources

Card Set A (for Teacher)

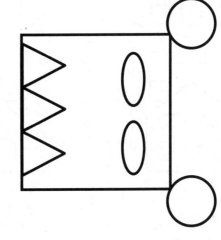

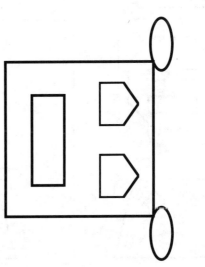

Card Set B (for Teacher)

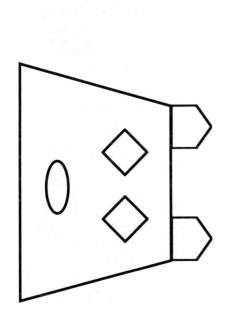

Name: _____   Date: _____

Alien Cards

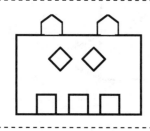 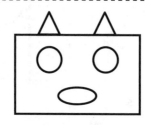 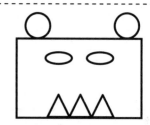

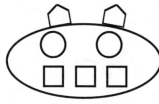  

  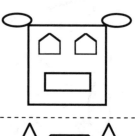

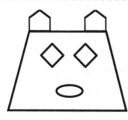 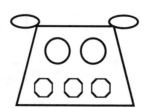 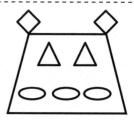

Reteaching Math: Geometry & Measurement © 2008 by Bob Krech, Scholastic Teaching Resources

Name: _____ Date: _____

WORD PROBLEM

Tracy is a shape made with three lines and three angles. She is 2-Dimensional. What shape is Tracy?

BASICS BOX

Tracy is a triangle. Triangles are simple 2-Dimensional shapes made with three lines and three angles (or corners). Triangles can have three sides that are equal in length, two equal sides, or no equal sides.

Basic 2-Dimensional Shapes

circle	oval	triangle	square	rectangle	rhombus

trapezoid	pentagon	hexagon	octagon

PRACTICE

1. Write the name of each shape on the line beneath it.

    _____   _____   _____   _____

2. I am a four-sided shape. I am a special rectangle because all of my sides are the same length. I have four right angles. What am I? _____

JOURNAL

Choose one of the shapes below and write a riddle about it.

pentagon   circle   hexagon   triangle

Name: _____ Date: _____

Write the name of each 2-Dimensional shape.

1.

   _____

2.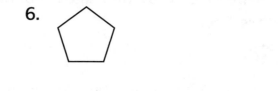

   _____

3. ◯

   _____

4. ▭

   _____

5. △

   _____

6.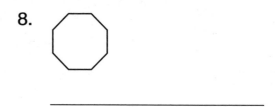

   _____

7. ⬡

   _____

8. ⯃

   _____

9. ⏢

   _____

10. ▱

   _____

Reteaching Math: Geometry & Measurement © 2008 by Bob Krech, Scholastic Teaching Resources

Name: _____   Date: _____

2-D Shape Handbook

_____

_____

_____

_____

_____

_____

_____

Reteaching Math: Geometry & Measurement © 2008 by Bob Krech, Scholastic Teaching Resources

Name: _____   Date: _____

Polygons

(closed figures whose sides are all line segments)

Polygons

Not Polygons

(curved or not closed shapes)

Polygons are named by the number of sides that they have.

triangle	quadrilateral	pentagon	hexagon	octagon
3 sides	4 sides	5 sides	6 sides	8 sides

Reteaching Math: Geometry & Measurement © 2008 by Bob Krech, Scholastic Teaching Resources

Name: _____   Date: _____

Quadrilaterals
(4-sided polygons)

Parallelogram
(two pairs of sides, the same length and parallel)

Kite
(two pairs of adjacent sides that are equal in length, with no parallel sides)

Trapezoid
(one pair of parallel sides)

rhombus
(all four sides, "both pairs," are the same length and parallel)

rectangle
(four right angles or square corners)

square

diamond

Reteaching Math: Geometry & Measurement © 2008 by Bob Krech, Scholastic Teaching Resources

Name: _____   Date: _____

WORD PROBLEM

Mariah was working on a shape dictionary in Writer's Workshop. She was working on the definition of a rhombus. She wrote: A rhombus is a closed shape. It is a quadrilateral, and all four sides are the same length. Although Mariah knew she was correct, her definition could also describe a square. What could Mariah add to her definition to make it better?

BASICS BOX

Both a rhombus and a square are closed shapes. They have four sides, making them quadrilaterals. Both a square and a rhombus have 4 straight sides of equal length.

The difference is that a square has four square corners, or right angles. Mariah could add that a square is a special kind of rhombus. Not every rhombus has four square corners, or right angles.

PRACTICE

Write the name of each shape after its description.

1. I am made up of all straight lines. I have 5 sides and 5 angles. A famous building is named after me. _____

2. I have no straight lines. I am perfectly round. If you draw a line from my center to any point around my shape, it will be equidistant (or the same distance). Clock faces and dishes are often my shape. _____

3. I am a quadrilateral (or 4-sided shape). I have 2 longer sides of equal length and 2 shorter sides, also of equal length. I have 4 right angles (or square corners). Swimming pools and doors are often my shape.

    _____

JOURNAL

Choose one of the shapes below and make a list of things found in our world that are that shape. (Example: rectangle—table, big screen TV, etc.)

square   octagon   hexagon   triangle

Reteaching Math: Geometry & Measurement © 2008 by Bob Krech, Scholastic Teaching Resources

Name: _____   Date: _____

Write the name of each shape after its description.

1. I am made up of all straight lines. You will find me on a soccer ball.
    Floor tiles often take my shape. I have 6 equal angles and sides.

    _____

2. I am a quadrilateral. My lines are all straight. I am sometimes referred to by
    another name, which is also the name of a precious stone. I am a parallelogram
    (my lines run parallel.)

    _____

Write the name of two objects from our world that are shaped like a . . .

3. rectangle _____   _____

4. triangle _____   _____

Write the name of each shape.

5. _____

6. _____

7. _____

Name: _____   Date: _____

Shape Memory Cards

Reteaching Math: Geometry & Measurement © 2008 by Bob Krech, Scholastic Teaching Resources

Name: _____ Date: _____

WORD PROBLEM

Mrs. Lynch sent her class on a shape hunt. Whitney found a tile in the wall that was shaped like a rectangle and was larger than her hand. Lily found a lunch ticket that was also shaped like a rectangle. Paco told Mrs. Lynch that the girls found congruent shapes. Was Paco correct?

BASICS BOX

Paco was incorrect. Whitney and Lilly found **similar** shapes because they both found rectangles. Both rectangles had the same number of sides, four, the same number of angles, four, and were made with similar lines. They were not congruent because although they were the same shape, they were not the same size. The rectangular lunch ticket was much smaller than a rectangular tile in a wall. For shapes to be congruent, they must be the same shape and size.

These shapes are similar. They are not congruent.

PRACTICE

Look at the pairs of shapes below. Decide if they are **similar**, **congruent**, or **neither**. Write your answers on the lines following the pair of shapes.

1. _____

3. _____

2. _____

4. _____

JOURNAL

In your own words, explain the difference between similar and congruent shapes. Be sure to include illustrations of both with your explanations.

Name: _____   Date: _____

Look at each pair of shapes. Write **similar**, **congruent**, or **neither** on the lines to describe the shapes.

1.

_____

3.

_____

2.

_____

4.

_____

What 2-Dimensional shape is each of these objects?

5. a postage stamp _____

6. a checkerboard _____

7. a stop sign _____

8. a photograph _____

9. a sail on a small boat _____

10. a CD _____

11. a cell in a beehive _____

12. a dime _____

Name: _____   Date: _____

Pattern Blocks

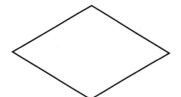

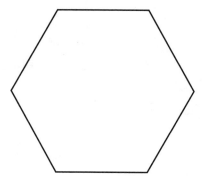

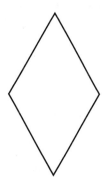
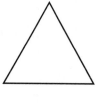

Name: _____   Date: _____

Master Shapes 1

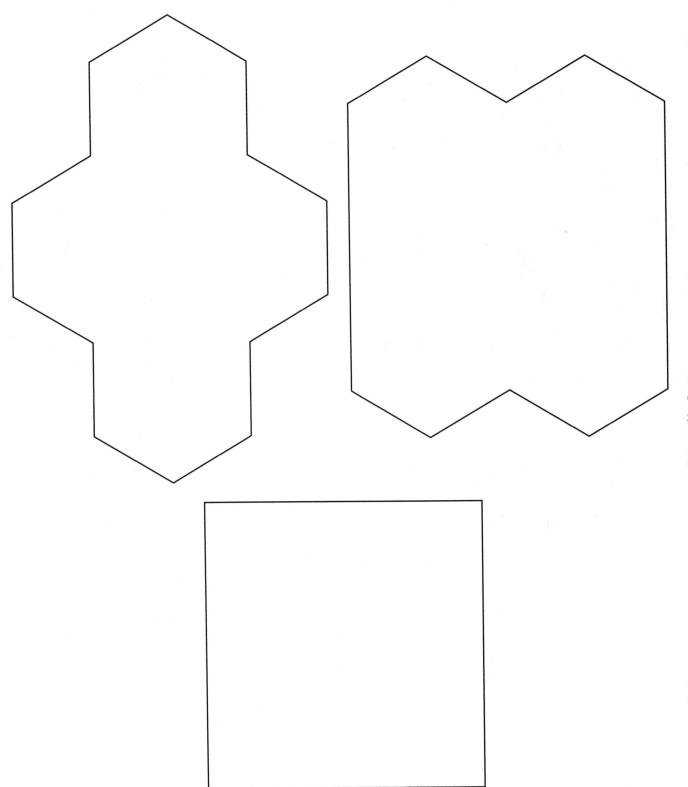

Reteaching Math: Geometry & Measurement © 2008 by Bob Krech, Scholastic Teaching Resources

Name: _____   Date: _____

Master Shapes 2

Reteaching Math: Geometry & Measurement © 2008 by Bob Krech, Scholastic Teaching Resources

Name: _____ Date: _____

Andrew was playing with pattern blocks. He used 6 triangles to make a shape with 6 equal sides and angles. He then used 2 trapezoids to make the same shape. What shape did Andrew create?

BASICS BOX

Andrew created a hexagon. A regular hexagon has 6 equal sides and angles. It looks like this:

With pattern blocks, a hexagon can be made using 2 trapezoids. It can also be made by piecing together 6 small triangles.

PRACTICE

Predict how many of each smaller shape it will take to cover the large shape. Next, cover the large shape with the appropriate pattern blocks and count. Record your predictions and actual counts.

1. Use: trapezoids

Predict _____

Cover _____

2. Use: triangles

Predict _____

Cover _____

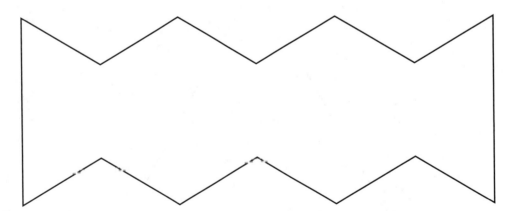

JOURNAL

Can you use only two pattern blocks to create a trapezoid? Prove it by using the actual pattern blocks to create the trapezoid. Then draw an illustration of what you made. Label the two shapes that you used.

Reteaching Math: Geometry & Measurement © 2008 by Bob Krech, Scholastic Teaching Resources

Name: _____ Date: _____

Put together and take apart shapes.

1. Cover the shape two different ways. Trace the pattern blocks you used to show your answers.

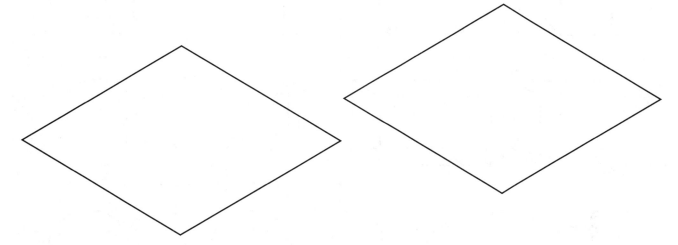

2. Cover the hexagon with pattern blocks. Use the remaining pattern blocks to make a congruent hexagon. Congruent shapes are the same size and shape.

Use these blocks:

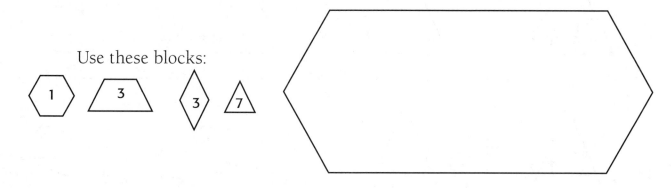

Look at the shapes below.

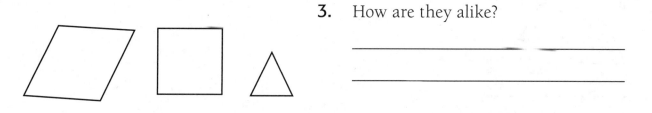

3. How are they alike?

_____

_____

Reteaching Math: Geometry & Measurement © 2008 by Bob Krech, Scholastic Teaching Resources

Name: _____   Date: _____

3-D Journal Shapes

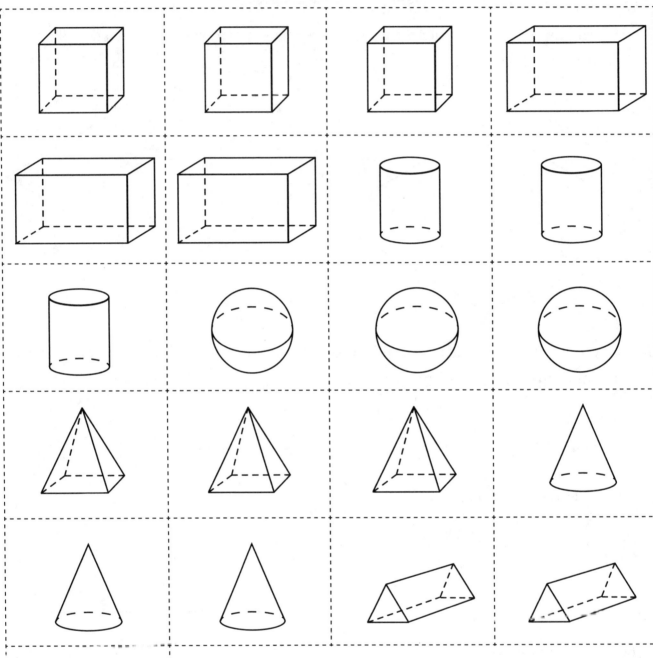

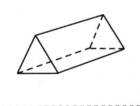

Reteaching Math: Geometry & Measurement © 2008 by Bob Krech, Scholastic Teaching Resources

Name: _____ Date: _____

WORD PROBLEM

Selfish Square had a birthday party. After cutting the cake into perfectly square pieces, the guests began playing a game called "Guess My Shape." Selfish Square lived up to her name and insisted on going first. "I am thinking of a shape with 5 faces, 8 edges, and 5 corners. You can trace its faces to create 2 different shapes. What is it?"

BASICS BOX

Selfish Square was describing a pyramid. A pyramid has 5 faces, 4 on the sides and one on the bottom. It also has 8 edges and 5 corners. If you trace any of the faces on the side of the solid, you will get a triangle. If you trace the face on the bottom, you will get a square.

pyramid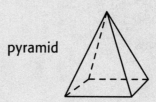

Basic 3-Dimensional Solids

| rectangular prism | cylinder | cube | cone | sphere | triangular prism |

PRACTICE

Write the name of each 3-D solid.

1. _____

3. _____

5. _____

2. _____

4. 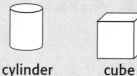 _____

6. 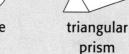 _____

JOURNAL

Choose one of the solids below and make a list of things found in our world that are that shape. (Example: rectangular prism—shoebox, brick, etc.)

cube   sphere   cylinder

Name: _____   Date: _____

Write the name of each 3-Dimensional solid.

1. _____

2. _____

3.  _____

4. _____

5. 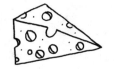 _____

6. _____

7. _____

8.  _____

Name these 2-Dimensional and 3-Dimensional shapes and solids.

9. _____

10. _____

11. _____

12.  _____

Name: _____   Date: _____

3-D Space Buttons

3-D Solid	Faces	Corners	Edges	Other Description	Idea for Button Action
cube					
sphere					
cylinder					
pyramid					
triangular prism					
rectangular prism					
cone					

Name: _____ Date: _____

Renee was using 3-Dimensional blocks to make a shape collage in Art. She was tracing the faces of the these blocks to create 2-Dimensional plane shapes. She traced around the face of a cube to make squares for her collage. Then she needed to make circles. Which block should Renee use?

BASICS BOX

Renee needs to use either a cone or a cylinder to create circles on her paper for the collage.

If Renee places a cone or a cylinder on its circular face, she can trace around it to create a circle.

PRACTICE

Write the name the 2-Dimensional plane shape or shapes you can create by tracing around the face or faces of each 3-Dimensional solid below.

1. pyramid _____ and _____

2. rectangular prism _____

3. cylinder _____

4. triangular prism _____

5. cone _____

6. Which solid cannot be traced to create a plane shape? _____

JOURNAL

Explain why a sphere could be put in the same category as a cone and cylinder. Include an illustration to prove your thinking.

Reteaching Math: Geometry & Measurement © 2008 by Bob Krech, Scholastic Teaching Resources

Name: _____ Date: _____

Which solids could be traced to create the plane shapes below? Write the names of the solids on the lines provided.

1. ☐ _____ and _____

2. ○ _____ and _____

3. ▭ _____ and _____

4. △ _____ and _____

Name these 2-Dimensional and 3-Dimensional shapes and solids.

5. _____

6. _____

7. _____

8. _____

Reteaching Math: Geometry & Measurement © 2008 by Bob Krech, Scholastic Teaching Resources

Name: _____ Date: _____

Symmetrical Shapes

Reteaching Math: Geometry & Measurement © 2008 by Bob Krech, Scholastic Teaching Resources

Name: _____ Date: _____

WORD PROBLEM

Samantha Symmetric collects alphabet magnets. However, she only wants letters that have at least one line of symmetry. Her friend, Lenny Letter, gave her four more letters to add to her collection: B, R, T, and H. Which letters will Samantha keep for her collection?

BASICS BOX

Samantha would keep the letters: B, T, and H. B and T both have one line of symmetry. The letter H has two lines of symmetry. R is not symmetrical, so Samantha wouldn't want it for her collection.

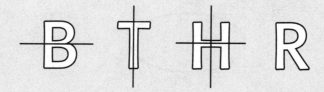

PRACTICE

Create each shape with pattern blocks on a separate sheet of paper. Then flip the blocks over the line of symmetry to make a "mirror" shape. Trace the blocks to show your work.

1.
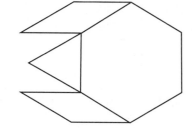

2.
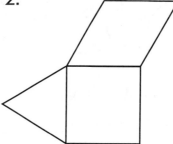

JOURNAL

Is the face of a human being symmetrical? Explain why or why not. Include an illustration to prove your answer.

Name: _____ Date: _____

Circle the shapes that have mirror symmetry. Put an "X" through the shapes that don't have mirror symmetry.

1.

2.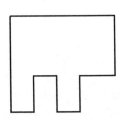

3.

4.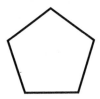

5.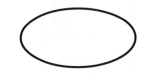

6.

Solve the shape riddles.

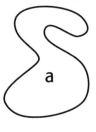 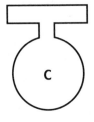  

7. I am partially round. I show mirror symmetry. I have corners.

   Which shape am I? _____

8. I do not have corners. I have at least 2 lines of symmetry.

   Which shape am I? _____

9. I have 4 corners. I have 2 pairs of equal sides. I have 2 lines of symmetry.

   Which shape am I? _____

10. I am a closed shape. I do not show mirror symmetry. I have no angles

    Which shape am I? _____

Reteaching Math: Geometry & Measurement © 2008 by Bob Krech, Scholastic Teaching Resources

Name: _____   Date: _____

Martian Mix-Up

1. _____

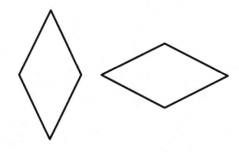

2. _____

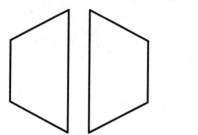

3. _____

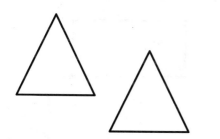

4. _____

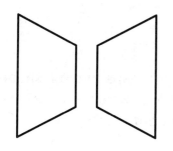

5. _____

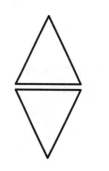

6. _____

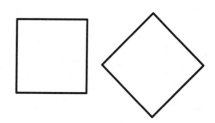

7. _____

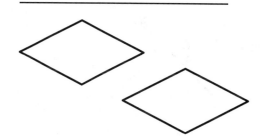

8. _____

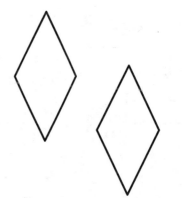

Reteaching Math: Geometry & Measurement © 2008 by Bob Krech, Scholastic Teaching Resources

Name: _____ Date: _____

Karen was creating a design in Art using a rhombus pattern block. Look at her design below. What did Karen do to the rhombus to create her design?

BASICS BOX

Karen **turned** her rhombus five times to create her pattern. She traced the rhombus each time she turned it. When you turn a shape, you rotate it around a point.

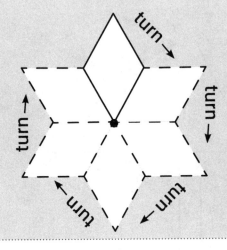

PRACTICE

Build each of the following shapes with multi-link cubes. Follow the directions to flip, slide, or turn the shape, then trace.

1. slide

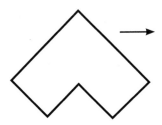

2. flip

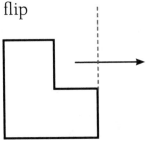

3. turn

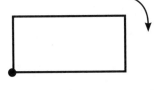

JOURNAL

Explain what it means to flip a shape and slide a shape. Be sure to include illustrations of both with your explanations.

Reteaching Math: Geometry & Measurement © 2008 by Bob Krech, Scholastic Teaching Resources

Name: _____ Date: _____

Look at each original shape or picture. Then look at the second shape or picture and decide if the original has been flipped, slid, or turned. Write: **flip**, **slide**, or **turn** on the line.

1. _____

3. _____

2. _____

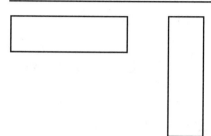

4. _____

5. _____

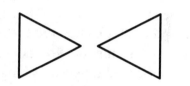

Circle the congruent shapes.

6.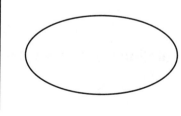

7.

Reteaching Math: Geometry & Measurement © 2008 by Bob Krech, Scholastic Teaching Resources

Name: _____   Date: _____

WORD PROBLEM

The students in Mrs. Sketch's Art class were asked to draw pictures with rotational symmetry. Below are examples from three of her students: Arthur, Amber, and Ocean. Who completed the assignment correctly? Who did not? Why or why not?

BASICS BOX

Arthur's Drawing   Amber's Drawing   Ocean's Drawing

Ocean and Amber completed the assignment correctly, but Arthur did not. Arthur's drawing shows mirror symmetry. Rotational symmetry is when an object is rotated around a center point a number of times, matching itself.

PRACTICE

Complete these designs using rotational symmetry.

1. 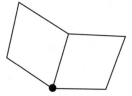   2.

JOURNAL

Explain the difference between mirror symmetry and rotational symmetry. Include illustrations of each with your explanation.

Reteaching Math: Geometry & Measurement © 2008 by Bob Krech, Scholastic Teaching Resources

Name: _____ Date: _____

Choose 2 different pattern blocks and create a design using rotational symmetry.
Trace the pattern blocks to show your designs.

1. Design A

2. Design B

Reteaching Math: Geometry & Measurement © 2008 by Bob Krech, Scholastic Teaching Resources

Name: _____

Date: _____

Luxury Lounge Floor Plan

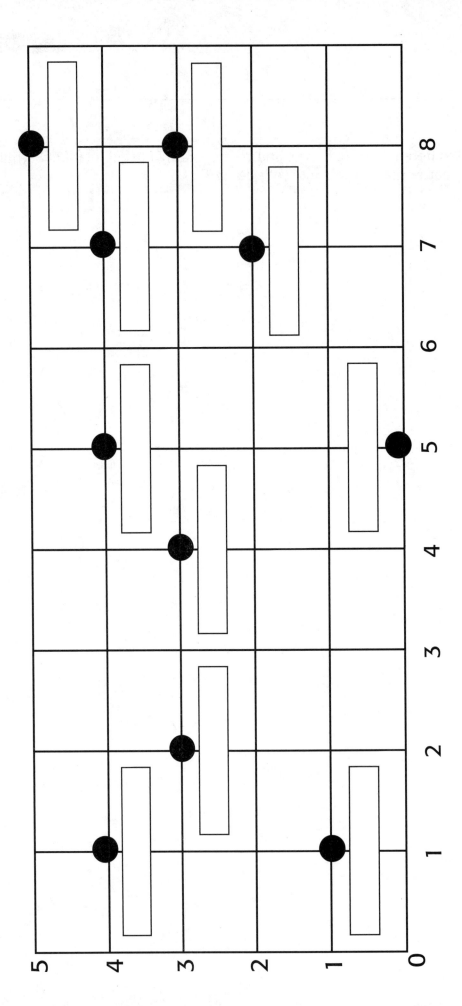

Reteaching Math: Geometry & Measurement © 2008 by Bob Krech, Scholastic Teaching Resources

Name: _____ Date: _____

Lounging Around Coordinates

Space Stations, Inc. needs your help planning the arrangement of a luxury lounge for the new space station. This lounge is an area of entertainment and relaxation for astronauts and alien space workers. Below you will find a list of ten objects that must be placed in the lounge. Use your floor plan to decide on the most sensible spot for each object. Label each object on the floor plan. Then, on the chart below, write the ordered pair for each object's location on the floor plan.

object	ordered pair (_____ , _____)
air hockey table	
beanbag chair	
bookshelf	
couch	
door	
reclining chair	
refrigerator	
snack machine	
stereo system	
wide-screen TV	

The lounge has room for 4 more objects. Decide what you think should be added to the lounge. Next, plot each object on the floor plan at one of the ordered pairs listed on the chart and label it. Finally, add the name of the object to the chart next to its ordered pair.

object	ordered pair (_____ , _____)
	(3, 4)
	(5, 2)
	(4, 1)
	(2, 5)

Reteaching Math: Geometry & Measurement © 2008 by Bob Krech, Scholastic Teaching Resources

Name: _____ Date: _____

Reteaching Math: Geometry & Measurement © 2008 by Bob Krech, Scholastic Teaching Resources

WORD PROBLEM

Derek was playing Treasure Hunt in his backyard. His mom had hidden a treasure and given him a map to help find it. The map was a coordinate grid and the starting point was (3, 2). "That's the jungle gym!" said Derek. Look at the map below. Was he correct?

BASICS BOX

Derek was correct. The jungle gym is located at (3, 2). With an ordered pair, the first number tells you how many spaces to move to the right, or along the bottom. The second number tells you how many spaces to move up, or along the side.

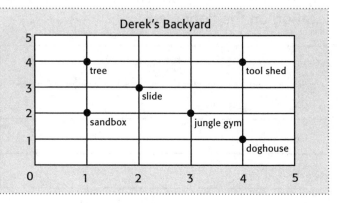

PRACTICE

Complete the ordered pair for the following locations on the coordinate grid map above.

1. slide (_____, 3)

2. tool shed (4, _____)

3. doghouse (_____, 1)

Write the ordered pair for each of the following locations.

4. sandbox (_____, _____)

5. tree (_____, _____)

6. Derek also has a sprinkler, a toy shed, and an apple tree in his backyard. The ordered pairs below show their location. Plot them on the map with a dot and label them.

a. sprinkler (3, 4)

b. toy shed (5, 4)

c. apple tree (0, 5)

JOURNAL

Write a definition for "ordered pair." Show a clear explanation with a picture, numbers, and words.

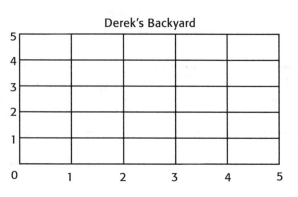

Name: _____   Date: _____

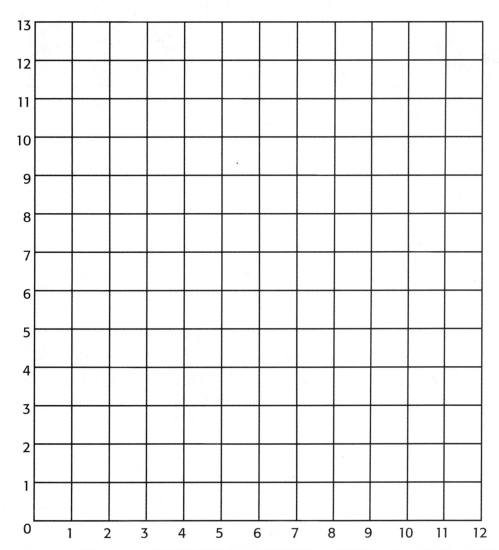

Use the grid to complete the following steps.

1. Draw a point at each ordered pair. (The first number shows how many spaces you move to the right. The second number shows how many spaces you move up.)

2. Label each point with the corresponding letter.

3. Connect the letters in order from A to Z.

4. What shape did you make? _____

ORDERED PAIRS	
A. (6, 13)	F. (6, 5)
B. (8, 9)	G. (1, 2)
C. (12, 9)	H. (3,6)
D. (9, 6)	I. (0, 9)
E. (11, 2)	J. (4, 9)

Super Space Stations, Inc.

Dear Students,

Thanks so much for your help so far with all of the space station tasks we have given you. Your skills with geometry have really come in handy.

Now we have more work coming our way. We hope you can continue to help us with these upcoming tasks. we will require assistance not only with geometry, but also with a great deal of measurement.

I look forward to continuing our work together as we create the best space stations in the universe!

Sincerely,

Ms. Ali On

President
Super Space Stations, Inc.

Reteaching Math: Geometry & Measurement © 2008 by Bob Krech, Scholastic Teaching Resources

Name: _____ Date: _____

Measurement Recording Sheet

Item	Estimate	Number of Units	Space Units
Width of a Doorknob			
Height of a Chair			
Width of a Bulletin Board			
Height of a White Board			
Width of a Desk			
Width of a Chart Stand			
Width of a Picture Book			
Width of a Stapler			

Name: _____ Date: _____

Molly was making pattern block bracelets by tracing pattern blocks onto foam craft paper, cutting them out, punching a hole, and stringing them onto a piece of yarn. Molly wanted to make a bracelet with triangles for her teacher. She cut the piece of yarn to fit her teacher's wrist and was now ready to make the triangles. Molly estimated that she could fit 7 pattern block triangles onto the piece of yarn. Look at the piece of yarn below. Is Molly's estimate too high, too low, or just right?

BASICS BOX

actual size:

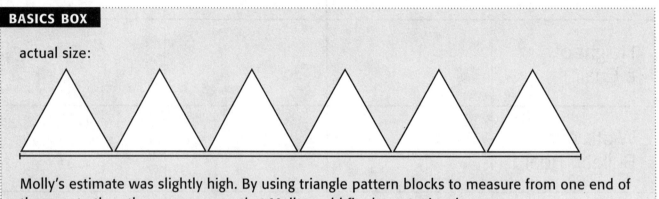

Molly's estimate was slightly high. By using triangle pattern blocks to measure from one end of the yarn to the other, you can see that Molly could fit about 6 triangles.

PRACTICE

Estimate the length of each line segment using the given pattern block unit. Then measure the actual length of each line segment using the correct pattern block shape. Record your estimate and the actual length.

1. pattern block unit: hexagon   Estimate: _____   Actual: _____

├───┤

2. pattern block unit: square   Estimate: _____   Actual: _____

├───┤

JOURNAL

Are there any problems with using nonstandard measurement?

Reteaching Math: Geometry & Measurement © 2008 by Bob Krech, Scholastic Teaching Resources

Name: _____ Date: _____

Estimate these lengths using the given nonstandard units. Then measure each object using an appropriate unit. Record both your estimate and the actual length.

1. nonstandard unit: triangle pattern blocks

   Estimate: _____ Actual: _____

2. nonstandard unit: square pattern blocks

   Estimate: _____ Actual: _____

3. nonstandard unit: small paper clips

   Estimate: _____ Actual: _____

4. nonstandard unit: crayons

   Estimate: _____ Actual: _____

Use pattern blocks to make a crab.

5. How many blocks does it take to make 1 crab? _____

6. How many blocks would it take to make 2 crabs? _____

7. How many blocks would it take to make 6 crabs? _____

Reteaching Math: Geometry & Measurement © 2008 by Bob Krech, Scholastic Teaching Resources

Name: _____ Date: _____

Reteaching Math: Geometry & Measurement © 2008 by Bob Krech, Scholastic Teaching Resources

WORD PROBLEM

Brad Braniac sat down to do his math homework. He needed to measure the width of his pillow, the length of his bedroom floor, and the height of his pencil cup in U.S. Customary units. Which units of measurement should Brad use to measure each object?

BASICS BOX

The smallest object that Brad has to measure is the height of his pencil cup. His pencil cup is definitely shorter than a foot, so inches would be the best unit of measurement.

The width of Brad's pillow would be less than a yard. It would probably be around a foot. Feet would be the best unit of measurement to use, along with inches for any remaining part of the pillow that is larger than one foot.

The length of Brad's floor requires a larger measurement, so yards should be used. Feet and inches may be needed for the remaining part of the floor that is not long enough to equal another foot.

PRACTICE

Choose the best unit of measurement for each object below.
Write **inches**, **feet**, or **yards** on the line.

1. the length of a football field _____

2. a piece of yarn for a bracelet _____

3. the height of a table _____

4. the length of a puppy _____

JOURNAL

Think about how measurement is used in our daily lives. Make a list of five ways people use measurement.

Name: _____ Date: _____

Look at each picture below. Estimate its length in inches. Then measure each picture to the nearest inch or half inch.

1.   Estimate: _____ in. _____ Actual in.

2.   Estimate: _____ in. _____ Actual in.

3.   Estimate: _____ in. _____ Actual in.

4.   Estimate: _____ in. _____ Actual in.

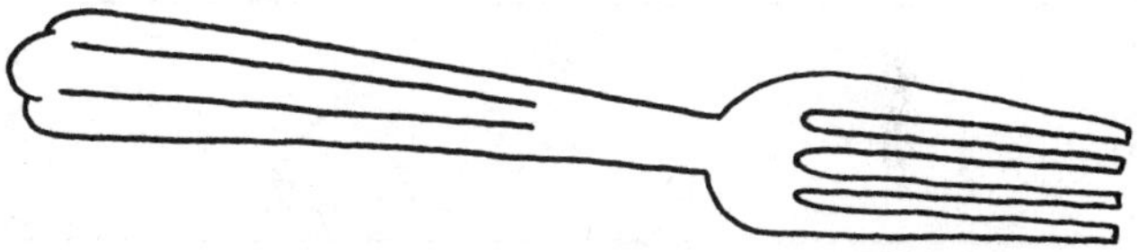

5.   Estimate: _____ in. _____ Actual in.

Circle the best estimate.

6.   the length of a pencil

    a. 6 inches

    b. 3 inches

    c. 10 inches

7.   the height of an adult woman

    a. 4 feet, 2 inches

    b. 8 feet, 3 inches

    c. 5 feet, 4 inches

Name the 2-Dimensional plane shape or 3-Dimensional solid shape of each of the objects below.

8.   an orange _____

9.   a cereal box _____

10. a soup can _____

11. an envelope _____

Reteaching Math: Geometry & Measurement © 2008 by Bob Krech, Scholastic Teaching Resources

Name: _____   Date: _____

Mixed-Up Measurement

Convert these mixed-up measurements to the most efficient units of measure. Marty mixed-up one final measurement. It was the measurement of the entrance to the space station. The mixed-up measurement is 78″. What is the most efficient conversion? How do you know?

Mixed-Up Measurements	Efficient Measurements
24″	
6′	
34″	
6′ 12″	
35″	
48″	
9′ 36″	
65″	
2′ 48″	
60″	

Reteaching Math: Geometry & Measurement © 2008 by Bob Krech, Scholastic Teaching Resources

Name: _____   Date: _____

Flurrytown was hit with three snowstorms in a row. On Friday night it snowed 5 inches. On Saturday it snowed 10 more. Sunday was the biggest snowstorm of the three; 20 inches fell to the ground. School was closed on Monday. How many feet of snow did the kids of Flurrytown get to play in on Monday?

BASICS BOX

The first step is to find out how many total inches of snow fell on Flurry town. By adding the snow amounts from Friday, Saturday, and Sunday, you get a total of 36 inches (6 + 10 + 20 = 36 inches).

The next step is to convert the number of inches into the larger unit of feet. To do so, you must keep in mind that 12 inches is equal to 1 foot.
12 + 12 = 24 inches or 2 feet, but the total has not yet reached 36 inches. Try adding another foot or 12 inches: 12 + 12 + 12 = 36 inches or 3 feet

The kids of Flurrytown had 3 feet of snow to play in. (This also equals 1 yard.)

PRACTICE

Convert the following measurements.

1.   12 inches = _____ foot

2.   _____ feet = 1 yard

3.   _____ inches = 1 yard

4.   48 inches = _____ feet

5.   9 feet = _____ yards

6.   72 inches = _____ feet

7.   68 inches = _____ feet, _____ inches

8.   _____ feet = 5 yards, 2 feet

JOURNAL

If Flurrytown had 2 more snowstorms and 10 more inches fell on Monday night, followed by 15 more inches on Tuesday, how much snow fell in total from all 5 snowstorms? Give your answer in feet and inches. Show your thinking using pictures, numbers, or words.

Reteaching Math: Geometry & Measurement © 2008 by Bob Krech, Scholastic Teaching Resources

Name: _____   Date: _____

Solve these measurement story problems. Show your thinking using pictures, numbers, or words. Remember to label your answer (example: 7 inches or 7 in.)

1. If Maiko is 5 feet tall, how tall is she in inches? _____

2. Peter is 10 yards from the supermarket. He is 30 feet from the video store. Is Peter closer to the supermarket, the video store, or is he the same distance from both? _____

3. Ferdie Furniture has a dining room table that is 72 inches long. How long is the table in yards? _____

4. Julia was the broad jump champion at Gator Elementary School. She could jump a distance of 65 inches. How far is that in feet and inches?

   _____

Measure each picture to the nearest inch or half inch.

5.  _____ inches

6.  _____ inches

7.  _____ inches

Reteaching Math: Geometry & Measurement © 2008 by Bob Krech, Scholastic Teaching Resources

Name: _____   Date: _____

Metric Materials

1. _____cm

2. _____mm

3. _____cm

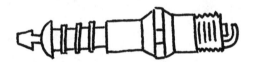

4. _____mm

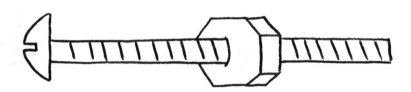

5. _____mm

6. _____mm

7. Draw an object that is 10 cm long.

8. Draw an object that is 40 mm long.

9. Draw an object that is 105 mm long.

10. Draw an object that is 4 cm long.

Name: _____ Date: _____

Christian's class was growing bean plants in Science. After one week, Christian drew a sketch of his bean plant's actual height in centimeters, below. After four weeks, the height of Christian's bean plant tripled. How tall was Christian's bean plant after one week? How tall was it after four weeks?

BASICS BOX

To measure the height of Christian's bean plant, you must measure from the tip of the tallest leaf to the base of the plant. Christian's bean plant was 4 centimeters tall after one week.

If the height of the plant tripled after four weeks, you need to triple the number 4. To do so, repeated addition (4 + 4 + 4) or multiplication (4 × 3) could be used. Both calculations will show that Christian's plant was 12 centimeters tall after four weeks.

PRACTICE

Measure the length of each picture below to the nearest centimeter.

1. _____ cm

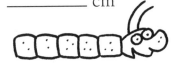

2. _____ cm

Measure the length of the picture below to the nearest millimeter.

3. _____mm

JOURNAL

Draw a bean plant of your own. Record its height in millimeters or centimeters. Then write a story problem about your bean plant's growth. Ask a classmate to solve it.

Reteaching Math: Geometry & Measurement © 2008 by Bob Krech, Scholastic Teaching Resources

Name: _____ Date: _____

Measure the length of each picture below to the nearest millimeter or centimeter. Label your measurements to show which units of measure you use.

1.  _____

2.  _____

3.  _____

What is the distance between the points?

4. _____ cm

5. _____ cm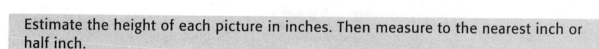

Estimate the height of each picture in inches. Then measure to the nearest inch or half inch.

6. Estimate: _____ in.

Actual: _____ in.

7. Estimate: _____ in.

Actual: _____ in.

Name: _____   Date: _____

Meter Space Exploration Model

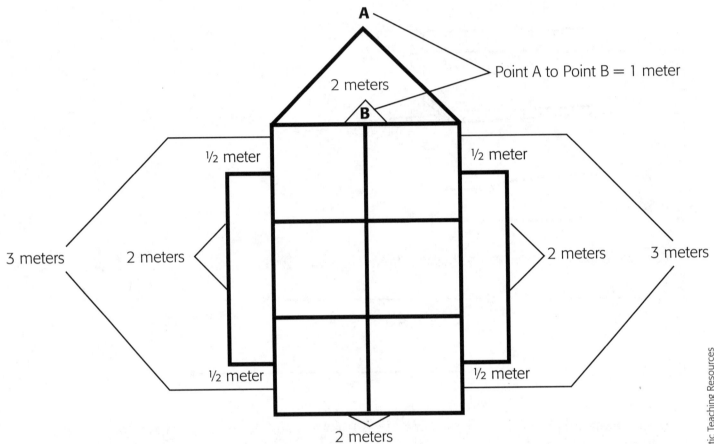

Super Space Stations, Inc. Space Vehicle

Reteaching Math: Geometry & Measurement © 2008 by Bob Krech, Scholastic Teaching Resources

Name: _____ Date: _____

Reteaching Math: Geometry & Measurement © 2008 by Bob Krech, Scholastic Teaching Resources

WORD PROBLEM

Jack is a member of the Sharks Swim Team and he is practicing for his swim meet on Saturday. Jack's team swims in an Olympic-sized pool. The distance from one end to the other is 50 meters. Which of the following could be the distance Jack swims in his race: 2,500 meters, 35 meters, or 400 meters?

BASICS BOX

Jack's race must be a distance of 400 meters. 400 can be divided evenly into 50. It would mean that Jack swims the length of the pool 8 times, or up and back 4 times. This would make sense for a swimmer.

2,500 meters is too far of a distance. It would mean that Jack swims the length of the pool 50 times, or up and back 25 times. Even for a long distance swimmer, this is quite far. Typically, the longest race is 1,500 meters.

35 meters is too short of a distance. It is not even the full length of the pool one way.

PRACTICE

Choose the best unit of measurement for each object below. Write millimeters, centimeters, or meters on the line.

1. the length of a pair of scissors _____

2. the length of a swimming pool _____

3. the length of a thumbtack _____

4. the height of a giraffe _____

5. the length of a car _____

6. the width of a book _____

JOURNAL

Why do you think that most of the world uses the Metric System? Do you think that the United States should replace the Customary System with the Metric System? Why or why not?

Name: _____ Date: _____

Estimate

1. Estimate the length of each classroom object below. Record your estimate, then measure each classroom object using a meter stick. Record your measurements.

Classroom Object	Estimate	Actual
the length of the chalkboard or whiteboard		
the width of the classroom door		
the length of your teacher's desk		
the height of a bookshelf		
the length of a table in your classroom		

Solve these measurement story problems.

2. Duncan and Noah had a contest to see which of their paper airplanes could fly the furthest distance. Duncan's plane flew 3 feet. Noah's plane flew 22 inches. How much further did Duncan's plane fly? _____

3. Goody-Two-Shoes, a kind but clumsy witch, was practicing magic spells. She was trying to make her pet cat, Kathryn, grow a longer tail, when she accidentally turned her into a mouse! Kathryn was now only 3 inches long! When Kathryn was a cat, she was 2 feet long, including her tail. How much shorter is Kathryn as a mouse? _____

Reteaching Math: Geometry & Measurement © 2008 by Bob Krech, Scholastic Teaching Resources

Name: _____   Date: _____

Metric Mix-Up

Convert these mixed-up measurements to the most efficient units of measure. Don't forget to label each unit.

Mixed-Up Measurements	Efficient Measurements
1,020 mm	
300 cm	
2,040 mm	
550 cm	
1,000 mm	
2,002 mm	
160 cm	
20 mm	

Marty mixed up one final measurement. It was the measurement of the vehicle landing pad. The mixed-up measurement is 235 cm.

1. What is the most efficient conversion? _____

2. How do you know? _____

Name: _____ Date: _____

WORD PROBLEM

Viren and Thomas had a frog jumping contest. Viren's frog, Fast Freddy, jumped 80 centimeters. Thomas's frog, High-Flying Herbert, jumped 600 millimeters. Which frog won the contest?

BASICS BOX

In order to compare the two measurements, they need to be in the same metric unit. Either the 80 centimeters must be converted to millimeters, or the 600 millimeters must be converted to centimeters. Either way, it is important to remember that:

10 millimeters = 1 centimeter

To convert the 600 millimeters into centimeters, you would need to know how many groups of 10 are in 600. You are really dividing 600 by 10. There are 60 groups of 10 in 600, so 600 millimeters is equal to 60 centimeters.

Fast Freddy, Viren's frog, won the contest. He jumped 80 centimeters while High-Flying Herbert only jumped 60 centimeters.

PRACTICE

Convert the following measurements.

1. 10 mm = _____ cm

2. _____ cm = 1 m

3. _____ mm = 1 m

4. 4,000 mm = _____ m

5. 900 mm = _____ cm

6. 500 cm = _____ m

7. 1,050 mm = _____ m _____ cm

8. _____ mm = 2 m, 20 cm

JOURNAL

Fast Freddy jumped 80 centimeters. How far is that in millimeters? Show your thinking using pictures, numbers, or words. Did Fast Freddy jump under or over a meter? How do you know?

Reteaching Math: Geometry & Measurement © 2008 by Bob Krech, Scholastic Teaching Resources

Name: _____   Date: _____

Solve these measurement story problems. Show your thinking using pictures, numbers, or words. Remember to label your answer (example: 7 centimeters or 7 cm).

1. If Stephanie swam 5,000 cm, how far is that in meters?_____

2. Marvin the Martian was making a control panel for the Space Station.
    He was told to make the panel 6 meters long. Marvin only had a centimeter ruler.
    How long should the control panel be in centimeters? _____

3. Michael found a snail in the grass. It was 7 centimeters wide.
    How wide was it in millimeters? _____

4. Sydney walked on her hands for a distance of 3,000 millimeters in gym class.
    Her gym teacher, Mr. Fit, wanted to record the distance in meters.
    What measurement should Mr. Fit record for Sydney? _____

Measure the length of each picture to the nearest millimeter or centimeter.

5. _____ cm

6. _____ cm _____ mm

7. _____ cm

Name: _____ Date: _____

Luxury Lounge: Area Directions

Directions

Use this map of the Luxury Lounge and all its furniture. Look at each piece of furniture and find its area using the one-inch grid to help you. Each square on the grid has one-inch sides. After calculating the total area, or measurement within each piece of furniture, write your answer. Remember that all the answers are labeled in **square inches**, the standard unit of measurement that you will be using today.

- -

Name: _____ Date: _____

Luxury Lounge: Perimeter Directions

Directions

Use this map of the Luxury Lounge and all its furniture. Look at each piece of furniture and find its perimeter using the one-inch grid to help you. Each square on the grid has one-inch sides. After calculating the total perimeter, or measurement around each piece of furniture, write your answer. Remember that all the answers are labeled in **inches**, the standard unit of measurement that you will be using today.

Reteaching Math: Geometry & Measurement © 2008 by Bob Krech, Scholastic Teaching Resources

Luxury Lounge ☐ Area ☐ Perimeter

Name: _____   Date: _____

bookcase _____

couch _____

movie screen _____

video game station _____

TV

_____

snack
table

_____

chair _____

game table _____

Reteaching Math: Geometry & Measurement © 2008 by Bob Krech, Scholastic Teaching Resources

Name: _____ Date: _____

Reteaching Math: Geometry & Measurement © 2008 by Bob Krech, Scholastic Teaching Resources

WORD PROBLEM

Preston's poodle, Petunia, is very fussy. She likes only the finest things. Petunia's paws are sliding on the floor in her Poodle Palace, and she has been very grumpy. Preston has decided to put wall-to-wall carpeting down to replace the slippery floor. If her Poodle Palace measures 6 feet long by 4 feet wide, how many square feet of carpet should Preston buy?

BASICS BOX

Drawing a picture is a helpful strategy for solving this problem.

□ = 1 square foot

If the Poodle Palace is 6 feet long and 4 feet wide, it can be shown in a drawing. Once the 6 square feet are placed across (for length), and the 4 square feet are placed up and down (for width), the remaining square feet can be filled in to get the total, 24 square feet. The answer can also be found using multiplication.

To find area, you multiply the length times the width. In this case, 6 x 4 = 24 square feet. Preston must buy 24 square feet of carpet for the Poodle Palace.

PRACTICE   Find the area of each shape in square units.

1. _____ square units

2. _____ square units

JOURNAL

Preston also wants to carpet Petunia's dog bed. If her rectangular bed is 5 feet long and 3 feet wide, how many square feet of carpet should Preston buy for the bed? Prove your solution with an illustration.

Name: _____   Date: _____

Find the area of each shape below.

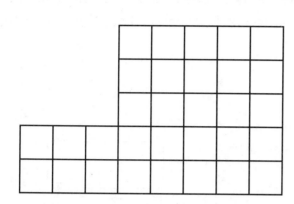

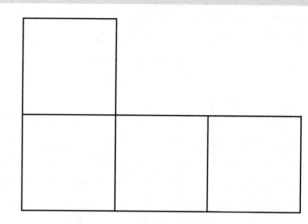

1. _____ square centimeters   2. _____ square inches

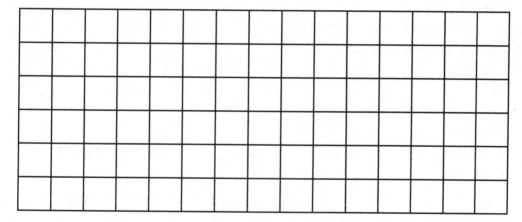

3. Create a shape that is 8 centimeters long and 5 centimeters wide. Record the area of your shape in square centimeters

Circle the best measurement for each of the following.

4. the length of a
   football field

   a. 100 yards

   b. 10 feet

   c. 500 yards

5. the wingspan of a
   monarch butterfly

   a. 30 centimeters

   b. 5 millimeters

   c. 12 centimeters

6. the length of an ant

   a. 4 centimeters

   b. 3.5 millimeters

   c. 10 centimeters

Name: _____   Date: _____

WORD PROBLEM

Ava Ant walked around the perimeter of a rectangular cracker at a picnic. Ava walked a distance of 28 centimeters. If the longer sides of the cracker were 10 centimeters long, how long were the shorter sides?

BASICS BOX

The perimeter is the distance around an object, so to find the perimeter of cracker, you would need to add up the distance of all four sides. With a rectangle, the two longer sides are the same length and the two shorter sides are the same length. If the longer sides of the cracker were 10 cm each, adding 10 cm + 10 cm equals a distance of 20 cm. The entire perimeter of the cracker was 28 cm. By subtracting the 20 cm from the total, you are left with 8 cm. That means the two shorter sides must equal a distance of 8 cm. When you split that evenly, you find that the shorter sides = 4 cm each.

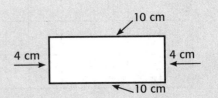

10 cm + 10 cm = 20 cm
28 cm - 20 cm = 8 cm left
4 cm + 4 cm = 8 cm
10 + 10 + 4 + 4 = 28 cm

PRACTICE

Find the perimeter of the shapes below.

1.
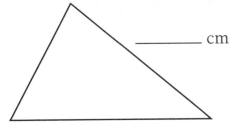
_____ cm

2.
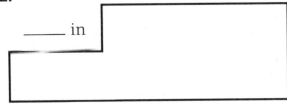
_____ in

Fill in the lengths of the missing sides.

3.
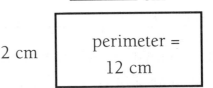
_____ cm

2 cm   perimeter = 12 cm   2 cm

_____ cm

4.
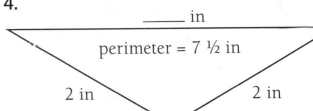
_____ in

perimeter = 7 ½ in

2 in   2 in

JOURNAL

Make a shape that has a perimeter of 15 inches. Label the lengths of all of the sides to prove that the perimeter equals 15 inches.

Reteaching Math: Geometry & Measurement © 2008 by Bob Krech, Scholastic Teaching Resources

Name: _____ Date: _____

Measure the perimeter of the shapes.

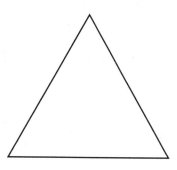
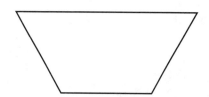

1. _____ centimeters   **2.** _____ inches

3. Create a shape that has a perimeter of 24 centimeters.
Label the measurements of each side.

Use one side of a triangle pattern block as 1 unit of length. Estimate the perimeter of the shape below, and record your estimate. Then measure the shape using the triangle pattern block, and record the actual perimeter.

4. Estimate: _____ units

Actual: _____ units

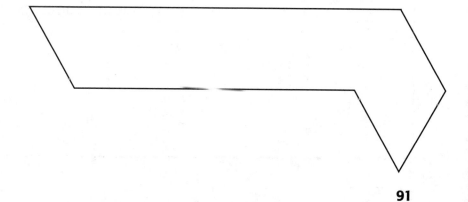

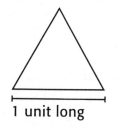

1 unit long

Reteaching Math: Geometry & Measurement © 2008 by Bob Krech, Scholastic Teaching Resources

Super Space Stations, Inc.

Dear Students,

   We are writing to thank you for all the help you have given us with the building and designing of our newest space station. Our space station is now ready for operation. We would like to thank you for becoming members of our planning committee.

   We greatly appreciate your commitment, effort, and math skills! As a result of your hard work, this space adventure was completed much more efficiently and skillfully.

   We are very pleased that you met the challenges we presented to you with such splendid success! Thank you again for your help and dedication.

Sincerely,

Ms. Ali On

President
Super Space Stations, Inc.

Reteaching Math: Geometry & Measurement © 2008 by Bob Krech, Scholastic Teaching Resources

Practice Page #2 (p. 35)
1. rectangle, oval, octagon, pentagon
2. square

Journal: Answers will vary.

Review Page #2 (p. 36)
1. square
2. oval
3. circle
4. rectangle
5. triangle
6. pentagon
7. hexagon
8. octagon
9. trapezoid
10. diamond/rhombus

Practice Page #3 (p. 40)
1. pentagon
2. circle
3. rectangle

Journal: Answers will vary.

Review Page #3 (p. 41)
1. hexagon
2. rhombus/diamond
3. Answers will vary.
4. Answers will vary.
5. triangle
6. pentagon
7. rhombus

Practice Page #4 (p. 43)
1. similar
2. congruent
3. neither
4. congruent

Journal: Similar shapes have the same number of sides and angles. They are the same shape but not the same size. Congruent shapes are the same shape and size.

Review Page #4 (p. 44)
1. similar
2. congruent
3. congruent
4. neither
5. square/rectangle
6. square
7. octagon
8. square/rectangle
9. triangle
10. circle
11. hexagon
12. circle

Master Shapes 1 (p. 46)
Answers will vary.

Master Shapes 2 (p. 47)
Answers will vary.

Practice Page #5 (p. 48)
1. 6 trapezoids
2. 18 triangles

Journal: The two blocks you can use are rhombus and a triangle to create the trapezoid.

Review Page #5 (p. 49)
1. Answers will vary.
2. Answers will vary.
3. These shapes are all alike because you can use the triangle to build them.

Practice Page #6 (p. 51)
1. cylinder
2. sphere
3. pyramid
4. cube
5. cone
6. rectangular prism

Journal: Answers will vary.

Review Page #6 (p. 52)
1. cube
2. rectangular prism
3. pyramid
4. cylinder
5. cone
6. cube
7. cone
8. sphere
9. pyramid
10. square
11. triangle
12. rectangular prism

3-D Space Buttons (p. 53)
cube: 6 faces, 8 corners, 12 edges

sphere: 0 faces, 0 corners, 0 edges

cylinder: 2 faces, 0 corners, 2 edges

pyramid: 5 faces, 5 corners, 8 edges

triangular prism: 5 faces, 6 corners, 9 edges

rectangular prism: 6 faces, 8 corners, 12 edges

cone: 1 face, 1 corner, 1 edge

Practice Page #7 (p. 54)
1. triangle and square
2. rectangle
3. circle
4. triangle and rectangle
5. circle
6. sphere

Journal: They are all 3-D shapes that you can roll.

Review Page #7 (p. 55)
1. cube and pyramid
2. cylinder and cone
3. rectangular prism and triangular prism
4. pyramid and triangular prism
5. cone
6. rhombus
7. triangular prism
8. trapezoid

Practice Page #8 (p. 57)

1. Answers will vary.
2. Answers will vary.

Journal: The general shape of a human face is symmetrical however there may be markings that are not, for example a birthmark on one side only.

Review Page #8 (p. 58)

1. symmetry
2. no
3. symmetry
4. symmetry
5. symmetry
6. no
7. c
8. b
9. e
10. a

Martian Mix-Up (p. 59)

1. turn
2. flip
3. slide
4. flip
5. flip
6. turn
7. slide
8. slide

Practice Page #9 (p. 60)

1. Answers will vary.
2. Answers will vary.
3. Answers will vary.

Journal: When you flip a shape you actually turn it over so the back of the original becomes the front. When you slide a shape you are only moving its location on the page.

Review Page #9 (p. 61)

1. turn
2. flip
3. slide
4. flip or turn
5. turn
6. The fourth shape is congruent.
7. The fifth shape is congruent.

Practice Page #10 (p. 62)

1. Answers will vary.
2. Answers will vary.

Journal: Mirror symmetry happens on shapes that can be folded to show two equal pieces. Rotational symmetry shows symmetry around a given point.

Review Page #10 (p. 63)

Answers will vary.

Lounging Around Coordinates (p. 65)

Answers will vary.

Practice Page #11 (p. 66)

1. 2
2. 4
3. 4
4. (1, 2)
5. (1, 4)
6.

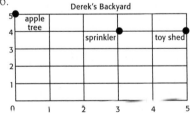

Journal: An ordered pair is a plot on a coordinate grid. The first number tells how far across to go. The second number tells how far up to go.

Review Page #11 (p. 67)

1.–3.

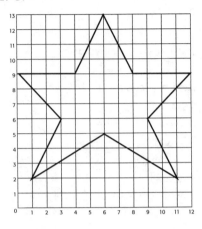

4. Shape: a star

Measurement Recording Sheet (p. 69)

Standard Units Activity: Answers will vary but should use standard units.
Metric Units Activity: Answers will vary but should use metric units.

Practice Page #12 (p. 70)

1. 3
2. 6

Journal: It isn't practical because if we use a form of nonstandard measurement not all people may have it available to them. If we need to share measurements with other people then they need to be standard so that everyone can measure using the same unit. This way we can get the same precise measurement no matter where we measure.

Review Page #12 (p. 71)

1. about 2 1/2
2. about 1
3. about 2
4. about 1
5. 4
6. 8
7. 24

Practice Page #13 (p. 72)
1. yards
2. inches
3. feet
4. inches

Journal: Answers will vary.

Review Page #13 (p. 73)
1. 2 inches
2. 1/2 inch
3. 1 1/2 inches
4. 3 1/2 inches
5. 1 inch
6. 6 inches
7. 5 feet, 4 inches
8. sphere
9. rectangular prism
10. cylinder
11. rectangle

Mixed-Up Measurements (p. 74)
2 feet
2 yards
2 feet 10 inches
4 feet
2 feet 11 inches
4 feet
12 feet
5 feet 5 inches
6 feet
5 feet

Practice Page #14 (p. 75)
1. 1
2. 3
3. 36
4. 4
5. 3
6. 6
7. 5, 8
8. 17

Journal: Answers will vary.

Review Page #14 (p. 76)
1. 60 inches
2. He is the same distance because 3 feet equal 1 yard so 30 feet is the same as 10 yards.
3. 72 inches is the same as 6 feet or 2 yards.
4. 65 inches = 5 feet, 5 inches
5. 5 inches
6. 2 inches
7. 1 1/2 inches

Metric Materials (p. 77)
1. 3 cm
2. 45 mm
3. 6 cm
4. 100 mm
5. 25 mm
6. 75 mm
7. Drawings will vary but should be 10 cm long.
8. Drawings will vary but should be 40 mm long.
9. Drawings will vary but should be 105 mm wide.
10. Drawings will vary but should be 4 cm wide.

Practice Page #15 (p. 78)
1. 4 cm
2. 7 cm
3. 30 mm

Journal: Answers will vary

Review Page #15 (p. 79)
1. 7 cm or 70 mm
2. 9.5 cm or 95 mm
3. 6.5 cm or 65 mm
4. 7 cm
5. 8 cm
6. 2 inches
7. 2 1/2 inches

Meter Space Exploration Model (p. 80)
Answers will vary.

Practice Page #16 (p. 81)
1. centimeters
2. meters
3. millimeters
4. meters
5. meters
6. centimeters

Journal: (sample answer) Most of the world uses metrics because the system uses tens and groups of ten are easy to calculate. The U.S. should switch because it is easier to remember and calculate. The only problem is they would need to change so many things.

Review Page #16 (p. 82)
1. Chart answers will vary.
2. Duncan flew 14 inches further. (Students need to change 3 feet into 36 inches in order to find the answer.)
3. 21 inches shorter (Students need to change 2 feet into 24 inches in order to find the answer.)

Metric Mix-Up (p. 83)
Chart: (the bold conversion is the most efficient one)
1 meter & 2 cm/102 cm
3 meters
2 meters & 4 cm/204 cm
5 1/2 meters/ 5 meters & 50 cm
1 meter/100 cm
2 meters & 2 mm/200 cm & 2 mm
1 meter & 60 cm
2 cm
1. 2 meters & 35 cm
2. Answers will vary.

Practice Page #17 (p. 84)

1. 1 cm
2. 100 cm
3. 1,000 mm
4. 4 m
5. 90 cm
6. 5 m
7. 1 m 5 cm
8. 2,020 mm

Journal: 800 mm. You need to multiply 10 times the 80 cm to convert to millimeters. He jumped under a meter because 1 meter equals 100 cm. 80 cm is less than 100 cm.

Review Page #17 (p. 85)

1. 50 m
2. 600 cm
3. 70 mm
4. 3 m
5. 10 cm
6. 4 cm 8 mm
7. 8 cm

Luxury Lounge (p. 87)
Area Activity

bookcase: 4 sq in
couch: 6 sq in
video game station: 5 sq in
movie screen: 4 sq in
TV: 1 sq in
game table: 3 sq in
snack table: 3 sq in
chair: 4 sq in

Perimeter Activity

bookcase: 10 in
couch: 10 in
video game station: 12 in
movie screen: 10 in
TV: 4 in
game table: 8 in
snack table: 8 in
chair: 8 in

Practice Page #18 (p. 88)

1. 8 square units
2. 20 square units

Journal: 3 + 3 + 3 + 3 + 3 = 15 square feet or 5 x 3 = 15 square feet.

Review Page #18 (p. 89)

1. 31 square centimeters
2. 4 square inches
3. Shapes will vary but area should be 40 square centimeters
4. 100 yards
5. 12 centimeters
6. 3.5 millimeters

Practice Page #19 (p. 90)

1. 14 cm
2. 8 in
3. 4 cm & 4 cm
4. 3 1/2 in

Journal: Answers will vary.

Review Page #19 (p. 91)

1. 13.5 centimeters
2. 5 inches
3. Answers will vary but the perimeter is 24 centimeters.
4. 11 units